THE GEEZERS' GUIDE
TO COLORADO HIKES

The Geezers' GUIDE to Colorado Hikes

Stuart A. Schneck, M.D.

and

Ida I. Nakashima, M.D.

University Press of Colorado

© 2002 by the University Press of Colorado

Published by the University Press of Colorado
5589 Arapahoe Avenue, Suite 206C
Boulder, Colorado 80303

The University Press of Colorado is a cooperative publishing enterprise supported, in part, by Adams State College, Colorado State University, Fort Lewis College, Mesa State College, Metropolitan State College of Denver, University of Colorado, University of Northern Colorado, University of Southern Colorado, and Western State College of Colorado.

The paper used in this publication meets the minimum requirements of the American National Standard for Information Sciences—Permanence of Paper for Printed Library Materials. ANSI Z39.48-1992

Library of Congress Cataloging-in-Publication Data

Schneck, Stuart A., 1929–
    The geezers' guide to Colorado hikes / Stuart A. Schneck and Ida I. Nakashima.
        p. cm.
Includes index.
    ISBN 0-87081-655-1 (alk. paper)
    1. Hiking for the aged—Colorado—Guidebooks. 2. Colorado—Guidebooks. I. Nakashima, Ida I., 1923– II. Title.
GV199.53 .S36 2002
796.51'084'609788—dc21

                                                                    2001006550

Photographs by the authors
Maps by Bill Nelson
Design by Daniel Pratt

11 10 09 08 07 06 05 04 03 02   10 9 8 7 6 5 4 3 2 1

With love to Lisa, Chris, and Pat,
who have climbed farther and higher
than we ever could

Contents

Table 1—Summary of Hikes

Hike #	Page #	Starting Altitude (feet)	Elevation Gain (feet)	Degree of Difficulty	Round-trip Distance (miles)
THE DENVER AREA					
A. 5,000–6,000 feet					
1. Barr Lake State Park – The Gazebo Trail	33	5,100	0	Easy	3.31
2. High Line Canal – Quincy Avenue to Belleview Avenue	38	5,381	20	Easy	3.74
3. Chatfield State Park – The Heronry Trail	41	5,432	50	Easy	1.40
4. Chatfield State Park – The Chatfield Dam Trails	43	5,500	0	Easy	2.12–4.60
5. Waterton Canyon–Waterton Canyon Road	46	5,520	80	Easy	7.38
6. Bear Creek Lake Park – Bear Creek Loop	50	5,558	40	Easy	2.41
B. 6,000–7,000 feet					
7. Deer Creek Canyon Park – Meadowlark/ Plymouth Creek Trail	54	6,000	830	Easy	2.67
25. Roxborough State Park – The South Rim Trail	111	6,100; 6,200	475; 375	Easy; Moderate	3.00
13. Apex Park – The Apex Trail Loop	71	6,200	1,000	Moderate	4.13

Continued on next page

Hike #	Page #	Starting Altitude (feet)	Elevation Gain (feet)	Degree of Difficulty	Round-trip Distance (miles)
24. Roxborough State Park – Fountain Valley Trail	109	6,200	200	Easy	2.12; 2.37
26. Roxborough State Park – Carpenter Peak	116	6,200	920	Moderate	6.44
9. Matthews/Winters Park – Mt. Vernon Village Walk	59	6,300	200	Easy	1.15
29. Castlewood Canyon State Park – Creek Bottom Trail to the Castlewood Dam Ruins	125	6,300	100	Easy	2.56
8. Matthews/Winters Park – Dakota Hogback (Dinosaur Ridge) Trail	57	6,396	200	Moderate	1.20
27. Castlewood Canyon State Park – Bridge Canyon Overlook and Canyon View Nature Trail	121	6,400	100	Easy	0.20; 1.00
10. Lair O' The Bear Park – The Creekside Trail	63	6,500	50	Easy	1.32
11. Lair O' The Bear Park – Bruin Bluff Loop	65	6,500	250	Easy	1.58
28. Castlewood Canyon State Park – Lake Gulch Trail to the Castlewood Dam Ruins	123	6,600	100	Easy	2.40

12. Pine Valley Ranch Park – The Narrow Gauge Trail, etc.	67	6,900	250	Easy	3.71
C. 7,000–8,000 feet					
22. Reynolds Park – The Hummingbird and Songbird Trails	100	7,200	400	Moderate	2.70
14. Mt. Falcon Park – The Castle Trail	75	7,400	213	Easy	3.60
15. Mt. Falcon Park – Eagle Eye Shelter and The Tower Trail	78	7,400	450	Easy	2.44
16. White Ranch Park – Rawhide, Longhorn, Maverick, and Sawmill Trails Loop	82	7,500	300	Easy	2.44
17. Lookout Mountain Nature Center and Preserve – The Nature Trail	85	7,540	120	Easy	1.21
18. Alderfer/Three Sisters Park – The Three Sisters and the Brother Trail	87	7,600	210	Moderate	3.32
19. Alderfer/Three Sisters Park – Evergreen Mountain	91	7,600	936	Easy	4.56
23. Elk Meadow Park – The Painter's Pause Trail/Meadow View Trail Loop	104	7,600	510	Moderate	4.18
20. Meyer Ranch Park – The Lodge Pole Loop	95	7,875	361	Easy	1.97
21. Meyer Ranch Park – Sunny Aspen Loop	97	7,875	465	Moderate	2.38

Continued on next page

Hike #	Page #	Starting Altitude (feet)	Elevation Gain (feet)	Degree of Difficulty	Round-trip Distance (miles)
D. 8,000–11,000 feet					
30. Golden Gate Canyon State Park – Mule Deer Trail to Frazer Meadow	130	8,500	700	Hard	3.06
31. Indian Peaks Wilderness – Mitchell Lake	133	10,345	335	Easy	2.18
32. Chief Mountain	136	10,700	1,000	Hard	3.44
ROCKY MOUNTAIN NATIONAL PARK					
33. Cub Lake	140	8,080	540	Moderate	4.60
34. Arch Rocks and The Pool	142	8,155	245	Easy	3.40
35. Alberta Falls	145	9,240	160	Easy	1.20
36. Mills Lake	147	9,240	700	Hard	4.90
37. Bierstadt Lake	150	9,475	245; 566	Moderate	4.22
38. Nymph Lake	153	9,475	225	Easy	1.00
39. Dream Lake	155	9,475	425	Easy	2.14
40. Emerald Lake	157	9,475	605	Moderate	3.56
ASPEN					
41. The Rio Grande Trail	160	7,700	-100	Easy	2.62
42. Aspen City Walk	162	7,900	100	Easy	2.85

43. Hunter Valley Trail	165	8,350	425	Easy	2.82
44. Weller Lake Trail	169	9,300	300	Easy	1.40
45. Maroon Lake Scenic Trail	172	9,580	0	Easy	1.18
46. Crater Lake	175	9,580	596	Moderate	3.64
47. Lost Man Creek Trail	177	10,507	500	Moderate	5.38
VAIL					
48. Vail City Walk	182	8,150	0	Easy	3.18
49. Booth Falls	186	8,400	1,400	Hard	4.08
50. Piney River Falls	190	9,360	560	Hard	6.16
51. Shrine Ridge	194	11,089	888	Hard	4.20
BOULDER					
52. Sanitas Valley and Dakota Ridge Trails	199	5,520	440	Easy; Moderate	2.18
53. Enchanted Mesa/McClintock Nature Trails	203	5,730	430	Easy	1.79
54. Bald Mountain Loop	207	6,920	240	Easy	1.10
55. Green Mountain West Ridge Trail	209	7,544	600	Hard	2.80
56. Sugarloaf Mountain	213	8,441	476	Moderate	1.34

Acknowledgments

We thank John T. Reeves, M.D., Professor Emeritus of Medicine at the University of Colorado School of Medicine, for his valuable input on the physiology of altitude and of aging, and on medical problems associated with altitude.

THE GEEZERS' GUIDE TO COLORADO HIKES

Introduction

Does the world really need another book on hiking
in Colorado?

We think so, because no previous Colorado hiking guide has been written specifically for people over the age of 60. The year 2000 census emphasizes the significant increase in this age group, both nationally and in Colorado. Older hikers often have been led astray by the time parameters suggested in some Colorado trail guides. Listing the duration of a 4.70-mile one-way hike that gains 2,900 feet in elevation to the top of Buckskin Pass near Aspen as 3.0–3.5 hours, as one guidebook does, simply bears no relation to the reality of hiking for many people over 60. Most trail books appear to have been written for 20-year-old athletes whose idea of hiking consists of running up and down a mountain in the quickest time possible, usually wearing shorts and little else, no matter what the weather.

We are the "geezers" of the book title. Rest assured that the term is not derogatory; our children have used it for both of us in a playful, affectionate manner for decades. The term implies an old person, and chronologically we certainly fit the bill—our combined age is 150 years.

This book is aimed primarily at the older day hiker rather than the hardy backpacker and overnight camper. It will also be of value to the unacclimatized visitor to Colorado. We prefer day hikes because one of us, who grew up on a farm, had quite enough of lantern light and outdoor privies as a child. We both believe firmly that the warmth of home (or a motel or hotel), a hot bath and a massage, a good mattress, and a satisfying meal—preferably prepared and served by others—are the best means of rejuvenating a tired old body for the next day's hike.

Most hikes we describe are in the Denver area and nearby foothills, but we also include a number in Rocky Mountain National Park, Aspen, Boulder, and Vail that will get readers up into Colorado's beautiful high country. We provide tips that will enable readers not only to get to the top of the mountain, but to get there in good shape, neither nauseated nor exhausted, still able to speak pleasantly to their companions. We want our readers to get off the trail feeling so good that they are eager to go again the next day, instead of having to soak sore muscles for hours in a hot tub. More importantly, by following our simple suggestions, older or unacclimated hikers will have the opportunity to smell the flowers along the way, admire the scenery, and exult in a sense of well-being and accomplishment.

For several years, we have given talks to groups of seniors, assuring them that, in most cases, "you're not too old to hike." Many in the audience asked for information about suitable hikes; this book is a response to those requests. We have chosen hikes that fit, in a graded fashion, the physical capabilities of most older hikers. At tourist destinations, such as Aspen and Vail, we have encountered able but unacclimatized older adults, unfamiliar with the area, who embarked on mountain hikes far beyond their physical capacities. We believe that this group, as well as Colorado residents, will benefit from our hiking recommendations, which offer physiological and medical information to enhance an understanding of how older bodies function with effort at altitude.

To establish our credentials, and to encourage readers to believe that they, too, can follow in our footsteps (pun intended), we offer the following facts about ourselves. We have been hiking together in Colorado for more than 47 years and have hiked in Alaska, the Austrian and Italian Tyrol, the Scottish Highlands, the Faroe Islands, Iceland, and even an island off the coast of Antarctica. During this time, we probably have made and corrected just about every physiological mistake and judgmental error possible in hiking. Winter snowshoeing, too, forms part of our experience. One of us was involved with the medical care of seniors for more than 20 years and quickly realized the benefit of graded exercise for this group.

One author grew up on the streets of New York City. The other, having been part of a farm labor force, never associated physical exertion with pleasure. Between us, we have had part of a lung removed, mild anemia, asthma, hay fever, migraine, and a back that intermittently makes its weakness known. Despite these infirmities, we are certain that if we, properly conditioned, can hike 8–10 miles without exhaustion and achieve elevation gains up to 2,500 feet, so, too, can many of our readers.

Our overall purpose is to encourage older individuals, not necessarily in prime physical condition, who hike infrequently or not at all, to pursue this healthful, inexpensive activity in a manner that respects the physical limitations associated with age. Profiting from our experiences should allow the older hiker to enjoy the freedom, beauty, and exhilaration of Colorado's high mountain peaks and valleys. Hiking undertaken with respect for, and an understanding of, the limitations of our bodies can be thrilling. Hiking done otherwise can be frustrating, uncomfortable, and even dangerous.

The pleasure of hiking can be enhanced immensely by walking with another person, someone accustomed to your pace who doesn't mind stopping when you are out of breath, who is agreeable and sensible, and with whom there is no sense of competition. It is never a good idea to hike alone in the high mountains, for you can get lost or suffer an injury and need help getting out.

We do not believe that our way of doing things is the only, or perhaps even the best, way for all older hikers. However, it works for us, and we believe that it may benefit others. It is important to be active for physical and psychological reasons. Hiking in a sensible way fulfills us, and we hope it will do the same for you. For us, and we hope for others, the journey is as important as the destination.

Finally, some words about the format of this book. Most of these hikes we have taken together, almost all on multiple occasions. Every hike described has been done or redone from 1998 to 2001. We have chosen hikes specifically for seniors, deliberately leaving out several excellent routes that we deemed too difficult or even dangerous. Other hikes have been discarded because they simply were not very interesting. Hikes that we considered too high (above 12,000 feet) or too long (10 or more miles) have also been eliminated. The reader will realize, we trust, that we cannot guarantee that trails and landmarks in the future will be exactly as we describe them now. We all hike at our own risk, but one of the goals of this book is to minimize that risk.

To allow readers to select hikes commensurate with their physical ability, we have listed them by location in Table 1 according to the following criteria: starting altitude, elevation gain, degree of difficulty, and round-trip distance. We consider starting altitude and elevation gain the two most important parameters in determining effort when evaluating a hike; round-trip distance is somewhat less important.

The degree of difficulty is described as easy, moderate, or hard. Clearly, this is a personal judgment. A hike viewed as easy by one person might be considered moderately difficult or hard by someone else 10 years older. If we err in our assessment, we do so on the conservative side.

We give round-trip distances for our hikes, along with starting altitude and elevation gained one way. Readers should be able to estimate their own physical capacity, using these important parameters. A 6-mile hike at 9,000 feet that gains little altitude is likely to be less strenuous than a 4-mile hike from 10,000 feet that gains 750 feet in 2 miles.

Our round-trip times do not take into account additional time spent stopping and enjoying the scenery. They merely serve as a guide so readers can plan their outings appropriately. We are not competing with anyone, nor should you.

To give hikers the necessary information about where they are and where they are going, we provide simple maps and detailed descriptions for nearly every step of the way. The maps have not been drawn to exact scale, but are useful for general compass directions and orientation. We have measured each foot of every trail using a surveyor's Rolatape®. This has allowed us to say, using a hypothetical example, that "at 2.80 miles, you will come to a fork. Go left (east), and at 3.00 miles enter a conifer forest." Most occasional hikers we have encountered do not carry maps (although they should). Using our scheme, which records most twists and turns and view points on a trail, we feel that seniors are unlikely to get lost. We are aware also that readers are not likely to be carrying pedometers to measure distance. However, if you know that a fork was at 2.80 miles and that you enter a conifer forest at 3.00 miles, you can feel comfortable knowing where you are at any time.

USGS maps are listed for those who want more detailed data about terrain and adjacent geography. Other maps, such as those provided by Jefferson County for its Open

Space hikes, give easily assimilated local information and have the virtue of being free. Lastly, for most hikes, we have included a preface containing what we hope is interesting information about the route. We feel that this additional knowledge enhances the pleasure of the trip.

Some Aspects of the Physiology of Altitude and of Aging

There is practical value for older hikers in knowing the effects of altitude and aging on our ability to perform muscular work, because many of the most scenic hikes in the Rockies are above 8,000 feet. None of this information is meant to discourage the reader or dissuade anyone from hiking in our mountains. We believe that the more you know, the safer you will be.

Oxygen

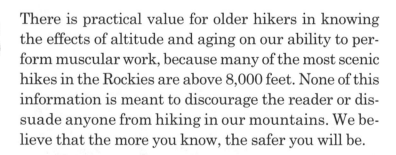

As we ascend, the air envelope pressing down on us becomes thinner. Oxygen is the most important component of our atmosphere, and as altitude increases, the pressure available to push oxygen into our lungs diminishes. As a result, the oxygen pressure in arterial blood (which gets this vital gas from the lungs), measured in millimeters of mercury, also diminishes. In young, healthy, nonsmoking adults, this pressure is 90 at sea level, 75 at Denver's mile-high altitude, 58 at 10,000 feet, and only 50 at 14,000 feet. Furthermore, as we ascend, the quantity of oxygen carried in the blood declines. At sea level, our blood is 98 percent saturated with oxygen. In Denver this saturation level drops to 92 percent, and in Leadville (10,152 feet) to 90 percent. On top of Mt. Evans, at 14,264 feet, oxygen saturation is only 85 percent. In short, as we go higher, there is less oxygen under less pressure in the blood.

Our body attempts to compensate for this relative oxygen deficiency, but it does so imperfectly, particularly during muscular effort. Lowered arterial oxygen pressure stimulates certain nerve reflexes to cause faster and deeper breaths (hyperventilation) in an attempt to move more oxygen into the blood to transport to working muscles. For reasons that are still unclear, low blood oxygen levels impair the ability of muscles to perform work. Exercise at altitude further lowers blood oxygen levels, and if the amount of exertion is too great for the body's compensation mechanisms, light-headedness, dizziness, and even fainting may occur. Studies of workmen building Colorado's Eisenhower Tunnel at 11,152 feet disclosed a maximum oxygen saturation of merely 80 percent, compared with the 90 percent found in healthy, sedentary young adults in Leadville only 1,000 feet lower.

Dr. Robert Grover, a former colleague, pointed out a number of years ago that "the most significant impact of high altitude is the reduction in man's capacity to perform muscular work." Every hiker, well conditioned or not, therefore must be aware that sustained work in the mountains (and hiking certainly qualifies) is less efficient than at lower altitudes.

The Heart

Though low blood oxygen is the major limiting factor in our ability to perform muscular effort at altitude, changes in the compensatory ability of the heart also play a role. The amount of blood the heart pumps each minute (cardiac output) changes with altitude. In Leadville (elevation 10,152 feet), healthy young people have a cardiac output reduction of nearly 20 percent even after a 10-day stay, and this reduction only increases with age.

Most of the preceding information is derived from studies of healthy young people, but it applies to older persons as well. Other physiological changes that occur normally in healthy older individuals further limit performance at altitude. The function of most body organs decreases by 1 percent per year after age 30. The maximum heart rate achievable in response to exercise illustrates this. A simple rule of thumb is that the maximum adult heart rate equals 220 minus age in years. Put another way, age decreases our maximum heart rate by about 10 beats per minute per decade. Thus, a 60-year-old hiker theoretically would not likely develop a heart rate much more than 160 beats per minute. An impressive demonstration is found in studies a physiologist conducted on himself. With maximal exercise at age 35, his heart rate rose to 168 beats per minute. At age 85, with the same amount and type of exercise, his heart rate climbed only to 112 beats per minute.

The efficiency of the heart as a pump also decreases with time so that a little less blood per beat is pushed out. By age 70, cardiac output usually has decreased by 20 to 30 percent. In addition, the resistance to flow in the blood vessels increases somewhat as we grow older, even in the absence of arteriosclerosis.

The Lungs

Age also affects lung function. The maximum amount of air that can be drawn into the lungs in a single breath is called the vital capacity, and this, too, decreases with age. Our lungs and chest wall become somewhat stiffer as we get older. A 60-year-old has to work 20 percent harder than a 20-year-old simply to overcome the elastic forces of the lungs and chest wall in normal breathing. Breathing rapidly (hyperventilation) due to activity, especially at altitude, requires an even greater effort. Age also decreases our ability to maximally increase our rate of breathing, just as it decreases our maximum heart rate. In summary, we lose about 40 percent of our pulmonary capacity between the ages of 20 and 80.

The Blood

Another important normal adaptation to lowered oxygen pressure at altitude is an increase in the manufacture of hemoglobin, the oxygen-carrying substance in our blood. In Denver, we have about a gram more hemoglobin per 100 milliliters of blood than do people at sea level. However, this increased production of hemoglobin also slows progressively with age.

The Muscles

The amount of human muscle mass also declines as we get older, and by age 65 has decreased about 20 percent. After age 35, muscle strength declines as well, more so in the legs than in the arms.

Since the body's work ability and efficiency decline with age, and fatigue occurs earlier the older you are and the higher in altitude you go, the lesson to be learned from these biological changes is that we older hikers must walk more slowly in the mountains than we once did, rest more frequently, and accept and understand our physiological limitations. Denial of these facts is not only foolish but potentially dangerous. Although work capacity, vital capacity, and maximum oxygen uptake at altitude improve somewhat with training, we cannot regain our physiological youth. To emphasize the effect of high altitude even on fit, experienced, young climbers, we point out that the first Americans to reach the top of Mt. Everest found that, despite using oxygen, they had to take a breath after every two or three words when speaking. Between each upward step near the 29,035-foot summit, they had to take seven breaths.

Medical Problems Associated with Altitude

To hike safely in the mountains, you should know something about the medical problems you might encounter. Rapid ascent and exposure to altitudes above 8,000 feet, especially for an unacclimated person, may produce uncomfortable and even serious problems. Please note that although we offer some information about medications, readers should always check with their own physician regarding the appropriateness of any drug for them.

Acute Mountain Sickness (AMS)

AMS is the most common altitude-related illness. Its most frequent symptom is a generalized headache, which develops in more than 50 percent of unacclimated people who ascend rapidly to 12,000 feet or higher. Some people, particularly those with migraine, may get an altitude-related headache at lower altitudes. Other symptoms of AMS are loss of appetite, shortness of breath, dizziness, weakness, and lethargy. The full manifestation of AMS usually takes a day or two to develop but can certainly occur earlier, especially if hard physical activity is performed. The headache can be quite severe and may be associated with nausea and vomiting. Because sleep diminishes breathing, leading to a further decrease in blood oxygenation at altitude, AMS symptoms may be acute on awakening. About 10 percent of all people venturing above 12,000 feet, even over a period of a few days, get severe AMS. For unknown reasons, some individuals are more susceptible than others. Even at the moderate altitude of our Colorado ski resorts, one study showed that 25 percent of skiers developed AMS within 36 hours of arrival.

The symptoms of AMS usually improve in a few days as acclimation occurs. However, the standard treatment for severe cases is descent to a tolerable lower altitude. You can avoid or minimize AMS by a gradual ascent (approximately 1,000 feet per day) to high altitude, rather than going to maximal altitude in a single day. To decrease their chances of developing AMS, lowlanders visiting Colorado might well consider spending two nights in Denver or Boulder before heading into the mountains. The same two-night delay in Vail, Aspen, and Estes Park would be useful for visitors who plan to hike much higher from those destinations. Less strenuous physical activity initially, good hydration, and avoidance of alcohol and sleeping medications also help.

A diet that derives at least 70 percent of its calories from carbohydrates, started one or two days prior to ascent, reportedly decreases the symptoms of AMS by about 30 percent. In ascents up to 14,000 feet, the prescription drug acetazolamide (Diamox®), begun 24–36 hours beforehand, has been found to be approximately 90 percent effective in avoiding or minimizing AMS. This medication is related chemically to sulfa drugs, so those allergic to sulfa may not be able to take it. The steroid dexamethasone (Decadron®) is also effective and can be used in a similar fashion by those unable to tolerate acetazolamide. A few recent studies have suggested that ginkgo biloba, a nonprescription herbal medication with fewer side effects than acetazolamide, also reduces the likelihood of developing AMS.

One benefit of age seems to be a somewhat lower incidence of AMS as compared to young people. A recent study of visitors aged 59–83 from all over the country who spent five days in Vail (elevation 8,150 feet) disclosed that only 16 percent developed AMS, even though 20 percent had asymptomatic coronary artery disease, 34 percent had high blood pressure, and 9 percent had lung disease. This suggests that persons with pre-existing but mild heart and lung disease can probably tolerate moderate altitudes (8,000–9,000 feet) safely without an increased risk of developing AMS or other altitude-related syndromes. To reassure Colorado visitors, we note that expert medical care is available near all the destinations covered in this book.

Dehydration

Dehydration can become a serious problem at altitude. Breathing hard and fast causes profound water-vapor loss from the lungs. Similar losses can occur through profuse sweating and evaporation from the skin. Weakness, nausea, vomiting, and confusion, as well as a drop in blood pressure, may result unless fluids are adequately replenished. For this reason, we advise you to drink frequently during your mountain hikes.

Hypothermia

Lowering of body temperature at altitude tends to occur more readily and insidiously in older people than in the young, not only in winter but in cool, windy conditions in summer. Sudden rainstorms pose a particular threat if a hiker is not properly dressed. The victim may experience confusion and drowsiness, trembling, irregular and slowed heartbeat, and low blood pressure. Rewarming is essential treatment, but prevention through wearing proper clothing is a much wiser policy.

Edema

Swelling of the face, hands, and feet, called edema, develops in some people, especially women. The cause is unknown. Edema is not prevented by gradual ascent or acclimation and may last for days or weeks in some who remain at high altitude. Acetazolamide and salt restriction may help. Full resolution occurs after descent.

High-Altitude Pulmonary Edema (HAPE)

HAPE, though uncommon in the Colorado mountains, is one of the most serious medical events that can occur at altitude and may cause death if untreated. More common in the young than in older people, it most often develops after rapid ascents above 9,000 feet and thus is often associated with significant exertion. Fatigue, shortness of breath, cough, and impaired or confused thinking are common symptoms, many of which worsen with sleep. The disorder can progress to coma, and death may occur 6–12 hours later. Some individuals are particularly susceptible to this disorder. Oxygen and immediate descent are necessary treatment. For severe cases, victims may require medication and the use of a portable hyperbaric chamber, called the Gamow Bag.

High-Altitude Cerebral Edema (HACE)

The brain may swell at high altitudes, a condition called cerebral edema, and if unchecked this may cause death. A few such cases occur annually in Colorado. Impaired thinking, decrease or loss of consciousness, and other neurological abnormalities may develop, probably due to a lack of oxygen in the brain. Administering oxygen and immediately returning the victim to a lower altitude are essential measures. Victims may also need dexamethasone and the use of a Gamow Bag.

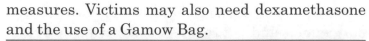

Retinal Hemorrhages

Retinal hemorrhages are very unlikely to occur during a day hike to the top of one of Colorado's fifty-four "fourteeners" but can occur after a stay of several days above 14,000 feet. Small retinal hemorrhages may not cause any symptoms, but larger ones may interfere with vision. Usually, these hemorrhages are absorbed without causing permanent damage.

Three other factors related to high Colorado altitudes deserve mention. Poor sleep quality and duration in the first few days after arrival are often experienced, particularly by older adults. The low humidity in the mountains may be associated with dryness of the eyes, especially during a prolonged stay. This may cause problems for those who wear contact lenses. Rarely, corneal ulceration may occur. Lastly, sudden, brief loss of consciousness (syncope) followed by rapid, spontaneous recovery has been observed both in healthy young adults and older adults.

For those interested in a more detailed survey of the medical aspects of hiking, including topics such as sunburn, sunstroke, and insect and snake bites, we recommend *Health Hints for Hikers* by Albert P. Rosen, M.D., himself a senior. This small book, published in 1994 by the New York–New Jersey Trail Conference, P.O. Box 2250, New York, NY 10116, costs only $5.95 and can be carried along easily on a hike.

The Benefits of Hiking

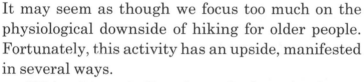

It may seem as though we focus too much on the physiological downside of hiking for older people. Fortunately, this activity has an upside, manifested in several ways.

Hiking is an excellent form of submaximal aerobic exercise. At just about any age, it produces increased strength, improves heart and lung function, and causes us to feel better generally. Regular physical exercise may keep the aging heart working like a younger one. A study of more than 17,000 Harvard alumni disclosed that, unlike light or moderate exercise, vigorous exercise is associated with an increase in longevity. With proper conditioning, we can go safely to many beautiful areas in the Rocky Mountains that are denied to the more sedentary, achieving an exhilarating sense of accomplishment. Nothing can compare with the sight of a high mountain meadow carpeted with spring wildflowers, or the sweeping vista of surrounding peaks viewed from a high mountain ridge. These experiences make all the effort worthwhile.

Though not yet definitive, evidence also exists that aerobic exercise improves several functions of the brain, including memory, comprehension, and abstract thinking (for example, the ability to do mathematics). Brain function declines for three general reasons: normal aging, about which we can do very little; disease, sometimes treatable, sometimes not; and disuse, certainly preventable by engaging mind and body, as we do when hiking. It is exciting to think that brain activity not only increases the connections between nerve cells but may actually increase the number of such cells, as recent research suggests.

The Hike

Preparation

Time spent on preparation pays big dividends in terms of the comfort, enjoyment, and success of any hike by older people. Though conditioning at low altitudes seems to have little value in preventing medical problems at high altitudes, it will increase muscle strength, limber up joints and muscles, and improve heart and lung function at any age. Conditioning through regular exercise may slow the rate of attrition associated with aging.

Any conditioning programs or exercises are useful if they increase heart rate to about 60–80 percent of maximum for at least 30 minutes three to four times a week. Obviously, a conditioning program is worth carrying on indefinitely, but you certainly should do it before hiking in the Rockies. An Austrian physician, Dr. Martin Burtscher, found that the risk of sudden cardiac death in mountain hikers was diminished in those over age 50 who exercised regularly. We have used a cross-country ski simulator and a stationary bicycle for many years, but swimming, using treadmills, and actual biking are equally effective. Hiking locally before tackling high trails provides clear conditioning benefits. If you have any medical problems, obtain clearance from your physician before attempting mountain hikes.

It may seem silly to point out that you should know where you want to go and how to get there before you start out. However, we are amazed at the number of people we have met who have gotten on a trail with no idea of its length, steepness, direction, altitude, and destination. You can get lost in the mountains quite easily on obscure trails, or get so tired that the goal becomes immaterial. We believe that a 3,000-foot ascent in a mile is usually too much for most older folks. Enjoyment in hiking comes from having a defined objective that can be achieved without nausea, headache, exhaustion, or argument, while you appreciate the landmarks, flowers, trees, and vistas along the way. This means that you will need a trail description, a map, or both, as well as a compass. U.S. Geological Survey maps are among the best. If we plan to do a series of hikes over several days, we leave the most strenuous for last so that we are most acclimated and conditioned when we attempt them. Starting out with a long, arduous climb often strains muscles, tendons, ligaments, and joints. The novice middle-aged or older hiker would do well to begin with short hikes and gentle ascents, then build up to the more demanding ones.

Over the years, we have refined the contents of our backpacks (see Table 2). We carry or wear plenty of clothing layers—sweater, windshirt, down jacket, wool hat (if you want to warm your body, put on a hat), gloves, and sun hat. Old bones chill easily, especially in winds and sudden squalls at altitude. We prefer to strip off clothing and carry it, rather than wishing we had a few extra pieces. For rain gear, Gore-Tex® or similar fabrics for jackets and pants are particularly effective. The March 2001 issue of *Consumer Reports* (pages 24–25) provides a good comparison of rain jackets. We use cotton clothing sparingly, for it holds moisture, and if the temperature drops significantly, wet cotton can have a significant chilling effect. A sweatband for the forehead is very useful. A cotton bandanna also absorbs sweat and doubles as a handkerchief, scarf, sling, or tourniquet. Be aware of how much you are sweating, for dehydration at altitude can be both rapid and subtle.

Food should be simple in preparation and lightweight. Our trail mix is a combination of raisins, nuts, granola, and M&Ms®. Oranges provide fluid, potassium, and easily assimilated sugar for energy. Sandwiches with margarine, meats, and cheeses are nutritious and easily digested. You can make your own dietary additions as you wish. Dehydrated foods sold commercially are useful but expensive. Emergency high-calorie foods include dehydrated bacon bars, granola bars, and mint cakes (glucose bars). Some hikers like to carry small cooking stoves to brew hot drinks or

Table 2—What to Pack for a Rocky Mountain Hike

CLOTHING
Down jacket
Extra boot laces
Extra socks
Gloves
Poncho and/or waterproof
  rain jacket and pants
Sunglasses
Sun hat
Sweatband and/or bandanna
Sweater
Windshirt
Wool hat

FIRST AID
Ace® bandages
Adhesive tape
Alcohol preps
Antihistamine
Aspirin, acetaminophen,
  or ibuprofen
Band-Aids®
Molefoam
Personal medications
Sterile latex gloves
Sterile nonstick gauze
  pads (2x3")
Sunscreen
Superglue®
Safety pins
Triangular bandage

FOOD
Electrolyte drinks (such as
  Gatorade®)
Food and Water
Oranges

HIKING AIDS
Binoculars
Bird, flower, and geology
  books
Compass
Forceps
Insect repellant
Maps
Moist towelette packs
Trail guides
Walking sticks

SURVIVAL GEAR
Cell phone
Duct tape
Emergency high-calorie foods
Folding scissors
Gorp
Iodine tablets
Multibladed jackknife
Pen or pencil and paper
Toilet paper
Water—more than you think
  you'll need
Water microfilter/purifier
Waterproof and stormproof
  matches
Whistle

soups or to sterilize water, but we have done this only when snowshoeing. We do not take alcohol of any type, because the expansion of blood vessels it produces often causes a headache. We always take plenty of water. For a very short hike, we each carry a quart, either in a canteen or a bottle carrier, but much more should be taken on longer hikes, particularly on a hot day. Some people may prefer electrolyte drinks such as Gatorade® or Powerade®.

It is also a good idea to carry a water microfilter/purifier or chemical purification tablets. Iodine tablets of several types are the most convenient option. Labels indicate the organisms, such as *Giardia,* that can be eliminated and the time and temperature necessary for optimal effectiveness.

We carry appropriate maps and trail guides on all our hikes, as well as lightweight flower, bird, and geology books. When hiking in the Tyrol, we were impressed with the number of hikers who used one or two walking sticks for balance or support. We find these sticks quite helpful, especially on steep grades. They are especially valuable in minimizing mechanical stresses on the knees. Moleskin is effective in preventing blisters.

Well-fitting and comfortable hiking boots, not sneakers, are mandatory, and waterproofing the boots frequently keeps feet dry on wet trails. You never fully appreciate your feet until you have hiked with blisters, wet socks, or ill-fitting boots. We use either a synthetic wicking sock and an outer heavy wool hiking sock, or thick and thin wool socks. Boots and socks should be of the best quality affordable for comfort and durability. One of us favors lightweight, waterproof Gore-Tex® boots; the other prefers heavier, sturdy leather boots.

The reasons for carrying most of the first-aid articles we suggest are obvious. Superglue® is effective for closing small, uninfected cuts. Nonstick gauze pads are comfortable to change if you have a bloody cut or badly scraped area. Clear adhesive tape allows you to see the lips of cuts. A triangular bandage can be used as a sling to support a limb, particularly a fracture or dislocation of an upper extremity. Secure this, or an Ace® bandage, with safety pins. Sterile gloves and forceps are useful when cleaning a wound. CPR knowledge is almost mandatory.

A cell phone may allow you to call for help in an emergency. Duct tape has an almost infinite variety of uses. Fully laden, one backpack weighs 10–15 pounds, and the other, 8–10 pounds.

Adequate sleep the night before the hike is essential for the older hiker. If you start out tired, exertion will only worsen your fatigue. "Early to bed and early to rise" is a good working maxim for the older hiker. Breakfast, with lots of calories and liquids, is essential to store up the energy and fluids that your body soon will need. You should feel pleasantly full but not stuffed; otherwise nausea may occur when you set out. Lastly, be aware of weather conditions. Hiking in rain or snow is often unpleasant and can be dangerous.

The Ascent

Choosing the starting time for any ascent is an important decision for mountain hikers. Obviously, you must estimate the duration of the hike, taking both length and steepness into account. We often add an hour to the time most trail guides list for a 3-mile hike at altitude, and an extra hour and a half for a 5-mile hike. In this guide, we list our actual hiking times, usually based on at least two trips. We urge you not to rush; we want you to have enough energy to finish in good spirits.

Knowing our own speed and capacity, we tend to hike as early in the morning as possible, especially in summer. That way we miss most other hikers, enjoy cooler temperatures (at high altitude, 2:00 P.M. can be quite hot), use less energy, and experience less dehydration because we sweat less. We also avoid the frequent afternoon mountain storms and can spend more time at our destination before heading down. We also confess that it feels good to be walking downhill when just about everyone else is struggling uphill during the heat of the day.

Stretching exercises just prior to setting out help muscles limber up—especially important if you have spent several hours in a car riding to the trailhead. We begin hiking at a very slow pace, allowing muscles and joints to warm up slowly and avoiding sudden muscle pulls. A walking rhythm soon develops that usually brings us our second wind in 30–60 minutes. Our pace may then pick up a bit if the terrain allows. We have learned that a rapid initial pace gets us hot, dehydrated, fatigued, sore, and pessimistic about the rest of the hike. The slowest in our party usually leads, thus setting a comfortable pace for all. Remember, we are not in a competition to get to the destination first. This is one reason we rarely hike with people much younger than ourselves. We still vividly remember the nausea and vomiting that accompanied a rapid ascent of Gray's Peak, 14,270 feet high, in the company of our then teenaged daughter.

We stop frequently, in the shade if possible, to catch our breath, which decreases dehydration due to water loss from the lungs and diminishes the risk of nausea and headache. Taking off your hat when resting speeds up cooling of the entire body. Taking one to two aspirin or Tylenol® an hour or so before a high-altitude hike and again after three or four hours if necessary often aborts headache in those susceptible to it. We resume hiking when we can speak normally without breathlessness, at which time our pulse has usually quieted down and no longer pounds. At these stops, we take in the scenery and enjoy the beauty of nature. Clothing is shed as needed to maintain a comfortable body temperature.

Every 30 minutes or so, we drink some water, and every 60 minutes we eat small amounts, thereby avoiding fatigue and dehydration. We don't take a lunch break per se, since waiting three or four hours for food may cause us to run out of energy. On a long hike, we might rest for 5–10 minutes every hour. Typically, we stand, because sitting tends to stiffen our muscles. Our hands swell frequently, probably due to gravity and the pressure of the backpack straps. We apply sunscreen liberally—very important at Colorado's high altitudes—to avoid sunburn and the general sense of malaise that accompanies it.

We cool ourselves whenever possible at mountain streams, again as an energy-conserving measure. However, we never drink mountain water, since an intestinal infection called giardiasis is commonly acquired from high-altitude streams soiled by animals and humans.

Boots, pack straps, and clothing may need to be adjusted along the way for comfort and to avoid blisters. You can get a good idea of your dehydration level (especially since water loss from sweating and breathing may be greater than you realize) by observing both the color and volume of your urine. A small amount of deeply colored urine should alert you to the need for increased fluid intake and perhaps a decrease in clothing to diminish sweating.

We have great respect for thunderstorms and their accompanying electrical displays in the high mountains, particularly on exposed ridges, and have elected at times to descend rather than chance a lightning strike. Colorado is one of the nation's leaders in the number of daily lightning bolts and lightning-related deaths. You need only have experienced one close strike of lightning, as we have, to become respectful of this awesome power of nature.

If what we have written sounds compulsive, we can only point out that we usually arrive at our destination feeling well and already anticipating the next day's adventure. During our early hiking years when we were learning what not to do, we rarely achieved our goals without a significant cost in energy and well-being.

The Descent

Returning to the trailhead calls for as much consideration as the ascent. Your legs and back experience an entirely different set of stresses and angles of force when going downhill. Toes, thighs, hips, and the front of your legs may announce themselves in new and painful ways. Retying your boots, placing your heels well back in them to minimize pressure on your toes, and holding your feet in place by tying the laces around the boot tops may offer some relief. Use a slow pace on the descent. Older hikers should take occasional rest stops, remembering to eat and drink, if they want to avoid hobbling to the car at day's end. The fastest downhill hiker should lead, so as not to step on the backs of a slower hiker's boots. Just as there is no rush to get to the top, there should be no rush to get down. Take time to smile at and encourage those still struggling upward.

In general, most of our hikes end between 1:00 and 3:00 P.M., in time for a hot shower or tub and/or a swim, followed by a refreshing sleep. We find that two or three days of hiking followed by a day's break before the next series keeps interest and anticipation high and muscle aches and pains at a minimum.

The Hikes, by Location

Barr Lake State Park

This tranquil bird and wildlife sanctuary is well worth a visit at any time of year. What began as a buffalo wallow and then became a trap for Denver sewage is now a 2,715-acre park containing a 1,900-acre reservoir. The presence of 346 species of birds, the most for any area of comparable size in Colorado, and 20 species of mammals makes this a wildlife-viewing paradise. It is one of the few areas near the Front Range that has successfully encouraged the nesting of bald eagles.

The reservoir, into which several private canals drain, is owned by the Farmers Reservoir and Irrigation Company, which manages it in cooperation with Colorado State Parks. The Denver and Hudson Canal along the eastern border of the park is also privately owned and maintained. The reservoir water is used primarily for downstream irrigation and secondarily for recreation. The park, operated by the state, opened in 1977, and recreational activities, such as wildlife viewing, hiking, waterfowl hunting, fishing, boating, horseback riding, and cross-country skiing, are available. Most trails are suitable for the handicapped.

A nature center near the south parking lot is an excellent place to begin and end a hike. Public educational programs guided by naturalists also start here. The center houses superb exhibits, including beautiful stuffed raptors, an informative display about the riparian community where water and prairie meet, and a small fish tank. Guided motorized tours for the elderly or handicapped on the Eagle Express originate here on spring and summer weekends beginning in May. The telephone number for information is (303) 659-6005. A daily or annual pass, discounted for seniors, is required to enter all Colorado State Parks.

The park is about five miles northwest of Denver International Airport. You can hear the roar of planes taking off and watch them glide gently in to land. By agreement, flights are not routed directly over the park.

Early spring is the best time to see nesting colonies of migratory birds and bald eagles and observe the courtship dance of western grebes as they run together across the water. In summer, the level of the lake begins to drop, mosquito numbers soar, and insect repellant is essential.

At this time, white pelicans fly and swim about, and egrets, cormorants, and herons are found in the heronry three miles south on the perimeter road. In autumn, when the water level is low, gulls, geese, and seasonal ducks, such as buffleheads, golden-eye, and cinnamon teal, are present. In winter, eagles and great horned owls roost in the cottonwoods, wildfowl swim in open patches of water, and red fox may be seen on the ice. A nine-mile perimeter road with short side paths to various boardwalks circles the lake. There are markers at one-mile intervals.

1. The Gazebo Trail

DEGREE OF DIFFICULTY: Easy
ROUND-TRIP DISTANCE: 3.31 miles
ROUND-TRIP TIME: 1 hour 20 minutes
STARTING ALTITUDE: 5,100 feet
ELEVATION GAIN: 0
MAP: Barr Lake State Park brochure

Barr Lake's exact altitude is open to debate. Four different trail guides list it as 5,280 feet, 5,100 feet, 5,096 feet, and "about 5,000 feet." A ranger told us it was 4,950 feet. Whatever the correct elevation, the park is somewhat lower than Denver. Another mystery, finally solved, involved the identity of the person for whom the lake and park were named. We now know that James M. Barr was a civil engineer who worked for the Chicago, Burlington, and Quincy Railroad, which constructed a line through this area in 1883.

Getting There: From northbound I-25, take the I-76 exit east toward Ft. Morgan. Stay to the left as you turn off to avoid being swept onto I-270, which exits to the right toward Limon. Drive 17.4 miles on I-76 to Exit 22 at Bromley Lane, just past a sign for Barr Lake State Park. At the top

THE GAZEBO TRAIL

Barr Lake

Nature Center &
Park Headquarters

Gazebo
Boardwalk

Denver & Hudson
Canal

✖	Trailhead
—	Gazebo Trail hike
- - - -	Other trails
═	Road
P	Parking
🛉🛉	Restrooms
◉	Scenic lookout

of the exit ramp (0.3 mile), turn right (east) at the stop sign.
Drive 1.0 mile. Turn right (south) onto Picadilly Road, just
past a sign for the park. After 2.0 miles on this dirt road,
make an abrupt right turn just past the park sign. The entrance station is 0.3 mile beyond, where a pass can be purchased. At 0.3 mile into the park, pass a road on the right
leading to the boat ramp and fishing access. Continue
straight, heading for the wildlife refuge and the nature center. The Cottonwood Picnic Area (with toilet facilities) is

0.4 mile farther on. An additional 0.3 mile brings you to the nature center. Picnic tables, drinking water, restrooms, and benches are located here.

The Hike: Begin at the bridge crossing the Denver-Hudson Canal. On the other side is the perimeter road, where you take a left at the sign for the Gazebo boardwalk. Almost immediately, pass a nature trail angling off to the right, named for Dr. Robert Niedrich, a naturalist and ornithologist. Take the boardwalk that leads out over a swampy area for a short distance. At 0.07 mile, the trail splits. Take the right fork toward the lake and adjacent cottonwoods. Enjoy fine views of the snowcapped Rockies across the lake if the smog is not too bad. A profusion of birds and waterfowl fill the air with their calls and songs. The multistoried building that stands out to the northwest is the Adams County Courthouse. At 0.19 mile, a wooden bridge crosses a marshy area and then the edge of the lake.

At 0.25 mile, there is a bench in a covered viewing area. The trail rejoins the perimeter road at 0.31 mile. Continue the hike by turning right (south). Farms, open fields, and some homes border the east bank of the canal. You will pass benches at 0.52 and 0.69 mile. At 0.77 mile, a sign indicates a small trail to the right, which goes 0.05 mile to a wildlife observation station. This small, very clean wooden structure with an inclined ramp serves as a viewing blind. Continue on the perimeter road as it begins to curve west. Another bench is located at 0.95 mile. At 1.04 miles, turn right onto the Fox Meadow Trail, which descends gradually to the lake and ends in 0.22 mile at another, similar viewing blind. The perimeter road is regained in 0.07 mile; from here you can see the gazebo.

Geese on Barr Lake.

At 1.62 miles, reach the gazebo path, where there is a bench and an enclosed portable toilet. A gentle descent leads to a boardwalk that ascends slightly and angles out over marsh and lake. About 45 minutes after starting, reach the gazebo at 1.80 miles. An information poster lists the trees bordering the lake (willows and cottonwoods) and frequently sighted birds (pelicans, great blue and black-crowned night herons, double-crested cormorants, eagles, Canada geese, and a wide variety of ducks). A free telescope affords good views of the mountains and wildlife.

The return on the perimeter road covers 1.51 miles from the gazebo to your starting point.

The High Line Canal

A favorite of Denver-area hikers and runners because of its easy access, the High Line Canal Trail also offers biking and horseback riding on a 58-mile, flat dirt road on which only maintenance vehicles are allowed. Owned by Denver Water, the path has been designated a National Landmark Trail. The canal itself, originally designed to supply drinking and irrigation water to land east of Denver, was completed in 1883 and now carries water intermittently for approximately 95 days a year from April through October. It begins about a mile from Waterton Canyon at the South Platte River and winds 71 miles northeast to its terminus east of the Rocky Mountain Arsenal. Large cottonwoods and wildflowers line its banks south of Hampden Avenue, 199 species of birds abound in trees and marshlands, and scenic views are frequent. In addition, 28 types of mammals (including the occasional mountain lion) and 15 rcptile species have been observed here. An informative Guide to the High Line Canal Trail can be purchased for a small fee from Denver Water. For information, you can telephone them at (303) 628-6526.

Our preferred canal hike is the section between Quincy and Belleview Avenues in Cherry Hills Village. The views west across a broad field, wetland, and lake just south of the Kent Denver School include the Front Range from south of Mt. Evans north to Longs Peak. Depending on the season, many Canada geese and varieties of ducks may be seen.

High Line Canal Trail—butterflies beware.

2. Quincy Avenue to Belleview Avenue

DEGREE OF DIFFICULTY: Easy
ROUND-TRIP DISTANCE: 3.74 miles
ROUND-TRIP TIME: 1 hour 10 minutes
STARTING ALTITUDE: 5,381 feet
ELEVATION GAIN: 20 feet
MAP: Not needed

Getting There: Drive to South Colorado Boulevard and Quincy Avenue and go east on Quincy for 0.5 mile to Dahlia Street. Turn right (south), pass the Arapahoe Tennis Club on the left, and at 0.3 mile down Dahlia, park in a wide dead-end area. Walk across a small wooden bridge over the canal to the trail.

The Hike: The route includes both of the following options; you may choose either one to begin with.

1. Turn left from the bridge and head southwest toward Belleview Avenue. You will pass benches at 0.15, 0.64, and 0.93 mile. At 0.25 mile, a sign identifies Blackmer Common (to the west), a designated open space containing a marsh. Walking in this 15-acre preserve is permitted. The hike mixes rural beauty with views of magnificent homes. At 1.33 miles, come to a tunnel going under Belleview Avenue. This point is approximately at mile marker 32.5 on the trail.

2. Turn right from the bridge and head northwest to Quincy Avenue. Benches are available near the trailhead and at 0.34 mile. At 0.30 mile, there is a large, private wildlife refuge, a pond with aerators and nesting boxes. No trespassing is allowed. Reach Quincy Avenue after 0.54 mile (mile marker 34.1 on the trail).

Trail signs put the round-trip distance at 4.30 miles, but our measurement was less (3.74 miles). If you wish to hike farther, a sign notes the distance from Quincy to Hampden as 1.50 miles one way, and from Belleview to Orchard Road as 2.60 miles one way.

Chatfield State Park

The Chatfield State Park area, named for Isaac Chatfield, an early settler, was home to mammoths and other now-extinct wildlife 150,000 years ago. A mammoth skull, said to be 100,000 years old, is exhibited at the Corps of Engineers Visitors Center adjacent to the park. Arrowheads and other artifacts found in this area indicate the presence of hunter-gatherer tribes several thousand years ago. The Cheyenne and Arapaho were residents in the 1800s.

When white settlers began building homes and businesses along Cherry Creek in 1858, the Native Americans warned them about major floods caused by storm runoff from the mountains. The settlers experienced this first-hand in May 1864 when waves 15 feet high swept through Denver, carrying away the city hall, other buildings, and a bridge, drowning 19 people. In 1885, floodwaters destroyed railroad bridges, and in 1933, Cherry Creek rose 11 feet in 45 minutes, again putting Denver under 15 feet of water. A dam finished in 1950 on Cherry Creek prevented Denver from flooding in 1965, despite stream flows exceeding those of 1933. However, flooding south and west of the city from the South Platte River, Plum Creek, and Bear Creek killed 13 people and caused damage totaling $300 million.

To restrain mountain runoff into the South Platte, state and federal authorities began construction of the earthen Chatfield Dam in August 1967. The dam, rising 147 feet above the river, was finished in 1977; the recreational area around the reservoir was opened to the public in 1975. At its top, the dam is 30 feet wide. The maximum width at its base is 1,500 feet. The Corps of Engineers Visitors Center, also called the South Platte Visitors Center, is a worthwhile stopping point for excellent exhibits, free area maps, and a wonderful view of the park and reservoir.

A series of walking trails, most paved and accessible to those with disabilities, winds around the reservoir. Horseback riding, boating and other water sports, camping, fishing, and picnicking are all available. There is even an area for flying model airplanes. A launch site for hot-air balloons is located near the Deer Creek entrance. Be aware that the park is quite crowded in summer, particularly on weekends.

Among the park's striking features are its great blue herons. From March to May, they used to nest in the cottonwood trees lining the southeastern shore of the reservoir. In recent years, however, many of the cottonwoods have died and fallen over, victims of high water and winter storms. In addition, about three or four years ago, cormorants and eagles pre-empted the nesting sites before the herons returned. These habitat changes forced the herons to nest farther south in the park, toward Kassler, where they are less easily viewed. Among the park's more than 300 avian species are great horned owls, belted kingfishers, osprey, red-winged blackbirds, double-crested cormorants, and the occasional bald or golden eagle.

Though hikers can begin walking anywhere on the trail that circles the reservoir for several miles, we have chosen two short, easy hikes as an introduction to this fine recreation area.

3. The Heronry Trail

DEGREE OF DIFFICULTY: Easy
ROUND-TRIP DISTANCE: 1.40 miles
ROUND-TRIP TIME: 30 minutes
STARTING ALTITUDE: 5,432 feet (altitude of reservoir)
ELEVATION GAIN: 50 feet
MAP: Not needed

Getting There: The park has two entrances. The main one is the Deer Creek Entrance Station. From the intersection of C-470 and Wadsworth Boulevard (Colorado Highway

121), go south on Wadsworth. If you wish to go to the U.S. Corps of Engineers Visitors Center, turn left at the second traffic light. Otherwise, for the park, continue south on Wadsworth to the next traffic light, a total of 1.1 miles since you exited C-470. Turn left and go 0.2 mile to the entrance station, where a daily or annual state parks pass can be purchased. Continue straight for 0.2 mile to a stop sign and turn right (south). After an additional 2.1 miles, cross a bridge over the South Platte River. At 3.0 miles, turn left into the Heronry parking area for the Heron Viewing Area Trailhead. Restrooms are available here.

The Heronry parking area can also be accessed via the Plum Creek Entrance Station. From its junction with C-470, head south on Santa Fe Drive (U.S. 85) 4.4 miles to a stoplight at Titan Road (Douglas County Road 7). Turn right and drive 2.2 miles to the Chatfield State Park sign at Roxborough Park Road (Douglas County Road 3). Make another right. You will reach the entrance station after 2.1 miles. The distance from here to the Heronry parking area is 1.2 miles.

The Hike: The asphalt trail, named for Frank A. Justice, offers views of nesting waterbirds and other wildlife, as well as a panorama of the foothills. The continuous sound of birds, particularly western meadowlarks, is interrupted only by an occasional train whistle.

From the parking lot, walk west toward the reservoir for a few feet, then begin walking south on the asphalt trail. At 0.10 mile, there is a wooden wildlife-viewing platform with informative signs about the area's prehistory and its twentieth-century floods. From here, the trail dips and rises gently. Benches are located at 0.25, 0.40, and 0.60 mile.

Just past the last bench, there is a second wildlife-viewing area near a handicapped-parking turnout. Signs here give information about local birds and mammals. Another 0.10 mile takes you to the last wildlife-viewing area, which has telescopes and information about great blue herons and double-crested cormorants.

Several dirt paths lead from the asphalt trail down to the water. If you wish, you may continue the hike south for several miles, across the South Platte and north on the western side of the reservoir. If not, retrace your steps to the parking lot. Group picnic facilities are adjacent (reservations are taken from May 1 to October 1).

4. The Chatfield Dam Trails

> DEGREE OF DIFFICULTY: Easy
> ROUND-TRIP DISTANCE: 2.12, 4.40, or 4.60 miles
> ROUND-TRIP TIME: 45 minutes to 1 hour 30 minutes
> STARTING ALTITUDE: Approximately 5,500 feet
> ELEVATION GAIN: 0
> MAP: Not needed

Getting There: You have two choices.

1. From the stop sign 0.2 mile beyond the Deer Creek Entrance Station, turn left toward the dam and drive 1.8 miles to the Chatfield Park Overlook parking area. Several picnic tables are immediately adjacent.

2. From the Plum Creek Entrance Station, drive 4.2 miles to the turnoff to the exit at the Deer Creek Entrance Station. Do not turn, but continue straight for 1.8 miles to the Chatfield Park Overlook parking area.

The Hike: A flat asphalt trail, marked by a sign stating "Public use is restricted to top of dam," runs along the top of the structure. Bikers and runners as well as hikers use

Chatfield Dam and Reservoir.

this path, which is closed to unauthorized vehicles. The views of the lake and foothills are beautiful. To the northwest, the Denver skyline rises against the horizon; to the southwest, the red sandstone formations in Roxborough Park stand out. Be aware that this hike often is very hot during midday in summer, and can be quite windy on a blustery day since it is totally exposed.

The 0-mile marker is just inside the barrier at the beginning of the path. From here, walk east for 0.30 mile until you reach a bridge to the spillway tower. The park authorities are serious about no trespassing here—the barrier to the bridge is ringed by concertina barbed wire. A dirt road veers away from the asphalt trail just before the

1-mile marker. At 1.06 miles, the path ends at a paved circle where two benches are located. Return the way you came.

If you want a longer hike (4.60 miles total), you can walk back from the paved circle to the turnoff of the dirt road and follow it southwest for 1.20 miles along the eastern border of the reservoir. A railroad track parallels the dirt road, with commercial de- velopment beyond it. This road ends as it crosses the track. Another dirt road, this one lower, also parallels the track and can be followed north. Additional views of the reservoir and foothills are the attractions of this extended hike. Return the way you came. If you walk on the asphalt path directly to the dirt road, follow it to the end, and return to the parking lot, the distance is 4.40 miles.

Waterton Canyon

This canyon road, an old railroad grade, is extremely popular not only with day hikers but with those hardy souls who wish to access the start of the Colorado Trail, 6.2 miles from the parking lot. Runners, bikers, and trout fishermen also crowd it on weekends. We found that in order to appreciate the beauty and serenity of the canyon, it is best to go during the week, and it is necessary to travel beyond the Marston Diversion Dam. This makes for a long albeit easy hike. Obviously, you can hike as much or as little as you wish. Like so many other foothills hikes, this one is also best avoided during the heat of summer.

In July 1820 the Stephen Long expedition recorded entry into what was initially called South Platte Canyon. The group camped in the area of present-day Kassler, previously known as Waterton, where the South Platte River leaves the mountains. The river water became extremely important to Denver's growth, particularly after 1879, when the High Line Canal began supplying water to lands east of the city. In 1890, the Kassler Treatment Plant started sending water to Denver.

The Denver, South Park, and Pacific Railroad, built by Governor John Evans, ran trains up and down the canyon to the Strontia Springs Resort, where bathers could soak in the hot springs and enjoy mineral-salt and vapor baths. The 243-foot-high Strontia Springs Dam, completed in 1983 near the start of the Colorado Trail, has created a 1.7-mile-long lake of 98 surface acres. Water from this reservoir is diverted through a 3.4-mile-long tunnel under the mountains to the Foothills Water Treatment Plant.

Waterton Canyon has more than 40 bird species and a herd of 20–35 Rocky Mountain bighorn sheep. In addition, mule deer, mountain lions, coyotes, bobcats, rattlesnakes, foxes, black bear, and the occasional elk have been sighted. Scrub oak, mountain mahogany, snowberry, mountain maple, chokecherry, ponderosa pine, mountain juniper, and Douglas fir grow adjacent to the river and on the canyon slopes.

5. Waterton Canyon Road

DEGREE OF DIFFICULTY: Easy
ROUND-TRIP DISTANCE: 7.38 miles
ROUND-TRIP TIME: 3 hours 30 minutes
STARTING ALTITUDE: 5,520 feet
ELEVATION GAIN: 80 feet
MAP: Not needed

Getting There: From the junction of C-470 and Wadsworth Boulevard (Colorado Highway 121), go south on Highway 121 for 4.6 miles and turn left onto Waterton Road. Proceed for 0.3 mile and turn left into a large, unpaved parking lot. From the lot, carefully cross Waterton Road to the trailhead, marked by four vertical yellow poles and a "Colorado Trail Trailhead" sign.

The Hike: At 0.05 mile, a signboard welcomes you to Waterton Canyon, the beginning of the 470-mile Colorado Trail. It contains a warning about falling rocks, rattlesnakes, changing weather conditions, rising water levels, and maintenance vehicles that drive the road. To protect the bighorn sheep and their habitat, no dogs are allowed in the canyon. A toilet is located at 0.09 mile.

The road passes through scrubby and grassy areas paralleling the river behind the Kassler Treatment Plant. At 0.12 mile, go straight across a large, paved parking lot to the dirt road on the other side at 0.24 mile. This wide road winds gently up into the canyon. At 0.51 mile, there are picnic tables under cottonwoods to the left. More may be found on the right at 0.62 mile. At 0.74 mile, note the 0.5-mile marker on your right (which does not include the 0.24 mile you walked to get to the mouth of the canyon). Pass more picnic tables on your left, and at 0.90 mile you will hear and see the river on the left. Early in the morning, birdcalls are quite noticeable.

At 1.18 miles, pass under large diversion conduit pipes. At 1.29 miles, there is a trail to a small fishing beach. The canyon becomes steeper here; the highest cliffs tower about 150 feet overhead. At 1.86 miles, note a large parking area on the left for the High Line Diversion Dam; adjacent there

The South Platte River, Waterton Canyon.

are several picnic tables set among willows and scrub oak. Reach a paved dip in the road at 2.17 miles, and at 2.42 miles pass a sealed mine entrance on the right. At 3.01 miles, there are picnic tables by the river, at 3.05 miles there are toilets, and at 3.11 miles there is an emergency telephone. Houses and utility sheds are located on the right. You will come to a spillway and the Marston Diversion Dam at about 3.40 miles. Here the river is higher, flat, and quiet. With the canyon rim about 100 feet above you, swallows wheeling about it in absolute silence, this is a lovely spot.

At 3.69 miles, there is another paved dip. A sign provides information about fishing regulations. A picnic table next to the river makes a good stopping place before retracing your steps to the parking lot.

Bear Creek Lake Park

Bear Creek Lake Park occupies 2,600 acres of what was once the floor of an ancient inland sea. The park was created when the Army Corps of Engineers built the mile-long Mt. Carbon Dam, completed in 1979, to prevent flooding from Bear and Turkey Creeks. (In July 1896, a Bear Creek flood rushed through Morrison and killed 27 people.) In 1982, the City of Lakewood and the U.S. Corps of Engineers signed a 50-year lease to manage this park for recreational purposes, which include fishing, boating, swimming, and windsurfing on Big and Little Soda Lakes as well as Bear Creek Lake. Picnicking, camping, biking, and horseback riding are also available. Not a Colorado state park, this facility charges a modest daily fee ($2 for seniors).

In our view, the hike that follows is strictly an early spring or late fall conditioner, since the park's location at the junction of foothills and plains is prone to very high summer temperatures. Those interested in birds will find hawks, owls, herons, cormorants, and a variety of songbirds. The visitors center has very nice exhibits and restrooms.

6. Bear Creek Loop

DEGREE OF DIFFICULTY: Easy
ROUND-TRIP DISTANCE: 2.41 miles
ROUND-TRIP TIME: 1 hour 20 minutes
STARTING ALTITUDE: 5,558 feet
ELEVATION GAIN: Approximately 40 feet
MAP: Bear Creek Lake Park brochure

Getting There: From the junction of U.S. 285 and C-470, head west on C-470 for 1.8 miles to the Morrison exit. Turn right at the Bear Creek Lake Park sign onto Colorado Highway 8, travel 0.6 mile, and turn right into the park. Turn left at the first stop sign after the entrance station and drive east 0.6 mile to the second parking area at Muskrat Meadows. There is a portable toilet here.

The Hike: The trail begins at the northeast corner of the parking lot and heads to the right past picnic tables and barbecue grills. At 0.04 mile, a horse trail angles down to the creek, but you go to the right, adjacent to the creek. At 0.16 mile, cross a bridge over Bear Creek and head left (east) through willow and scrub oak. A bench is located at 0.20 mile. At 0.34 mile, reach a fitness trail loop with many exercise stations. At 0.46 mile, go through a barrier at Station 11. Come to the crest of a small hill at 0.51 mile and

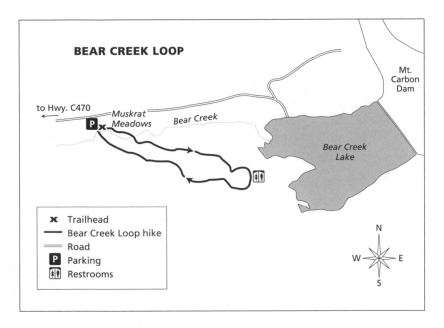

again go left (east). Cross a footbridge at 0.66 mile, pass through cottonwoods and elders, and continue beyond Stations 12–16, where there is a corral and stable to the right. At 1.26 miles (Station 18), there are toilets to the right. Continue straight, with the dam, lake, and a parking lot in front of you, and at 1.33 miles cross the start of the fitness loop. Follow the trail, which now heads west into a valley and toward the creek. Rejoin the creekside trail at 2.05 miles, walk upstream, and reach the bridge over the creek at 2.23 miles. Turn right (east) back to the starting point.

Hawk in Bear Creek Lake Park.

The following 17 hikes, located in Jefferson County, employ trails maintained by the Jefferson County Open Spaces Program. The program, begun in 1972, has developed a wonderful group of 18 foothills parks close to Denver, some of which have facilities for the handicapped. In 1999, they contained picnic tables, camping sites, historical points of interest, and 120.4 miles of trails, as well as areas for wildlife viewing, cross-country skiing, and fishing. These properties have been acquired, developed, and maintained with revenues from a 0.5 percent Open Space sales tax approved by county citizens. Maps of each park are available at Jefferson County libraries and at the parks themselves. Several of the parks offer naturalist-guided programs during the summer. The telephone number for Jefferson County Open Space information is (303) 271-5925.

We have selected some of our favorite hikes from the great number available.

Deer Creek Canyon Park

Before white settlers arrived, bands of Ute and Arapaho camped in the region. In 1872, Englishman John Williamson was the first homesteader, building a ranch and growing wheat, corn, and hay. The wife of the owner of the adjacent Couch Ranch befriended Chief Colorow and his Ute warriors, who then spared these ranches during raids against other settlers prior to the Ute removal to a Utah reservation in 1879. For a time, local mines produced quantities of gold and silver. Convicted man-eater Alferd

Packer lived here after his parole in 1901, and Jesse James allegedly stopped here for a time.

The park, part of Jefferson County Open Space, now comprises 1,881 acres—much of it from three of the original area homesteads—with 11 miles of trails. The Meadowlark, Homestead, and Golden Eagle Trails prohibit horses and bikes and are reserved for hikers only.

7. Meadowlark/Plymouth Creek Trail

DEGREE OF DIFFICULTY: Easy
ROUND-TRIP DISTANCE: 2.67 miles
ROUND-TRIP TIME: 1 hour 35 minutes
STARTING ALTITUDE: 6,000 feet
ELEVATION GAIN: 830 feet
MAP: Deer Creek Canyon Park brochure

Much of this trail is exposed to the elements and is quite hot during summer, even early in the day. No water is available on the way. The hike is best done in spring or fall. Its appeal is the fine view of the nearby meadows and valley below and the high plains beyond the hogback.

Getting There: From the junction of C-470 and Wadsworth Boulevard (Colorado Highway 121), drive south on Wadsworth 0.30 mile to Deer Creek Canyon Road. Turn right and drive 4.00 miles to Grizzly Drive. Turn left, go 0.40 mile, and then make a sharp right turn into the parking area.

The Hike: There is a signboard with an area map and brochure box. Nearby are restrooms, a telephone, and picnic facilities. The Meadowlark Trail heads off to the right (north). At 0.05 mile, a short trail on the right leads to several covered picnic areas with grills.

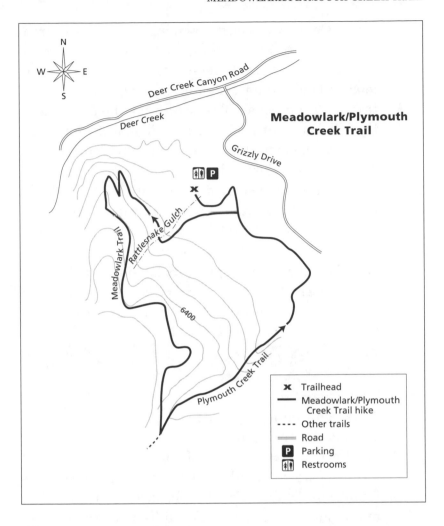

The trail now crosses and ascends Rattlesnake Gulch (appropriately named), switchbacking several times, with the last turn at 0.58 mile. The trail is now high above Deer Creek Canyon Road. Continue the gentle ascent, enjoying superb views to the east. At 1.04 miles, look west into Deer

Creek Canyon and east down into the parking area. Ascend and descend through profuse stands of scrub oak (uncommon in Jefferson County) that provide food and habitat for deer, elk, turkey, grouse, mountain lions, and bear. The trail hugs the east side of the hill. Due south is 7,200-foot Plymouth Mountain.

Near the mountain's top, cross Plymouth Gulch. The trail now descends to a bridge over Plymouth Creek (or its dry bed in summer) at 1.56 miles. Turn left and continue your descent through evergreens on the Plymouth Creek Trail. The trail is steep and rocky in places, so descend with care. The ravine to your left has whitish-gray rocks embedded in red sandstone soil. Signs marking the trail are found at 2.25 and 2.40 miles. Follow the trail back to the signboard area where you started.

Matthews/Winters Park

This easily accessible and historic park, part of Jefferson County Open Space, has 1,127 acres and 7.6 miles of trails. It is adjacent to the entrance to Mt. Vernon Canyon, one of the early routes to the Central City goldfields. The town of Mt. Vernon was founded in 1859 by Dr. Joseph Casto, a lay preacher and land promoter. He offered free lots to any takers, and by January 1860 the town had 44 registered voters. Jefferson Territory, with Mt. Vernon as its capital, was created in 1859 and lasted until the Colorado Territory was formed in 1861. Mt. Vernon faded into obscurity as Denver grew and other routes to the goldfields proved more popular.

We have combined two short and disparate hikes that are best done in the spring or fall to avoid intense summer heat. We suggest starting with the Dakota Hogback Trail but going only partway, since soon after reaching the Dinosaur Ridge Raptor Monitoring Station at the crest of the hogback, the remainder of the trail, an additional 1.5 miles, offers little in the way of new views to justify the effort involved. The raptor station is well worth a visit in the spring, since it is staffed by knowledgeable birdwatchers always eager to identify the different species that soar overhead.

When I-70 was cut through the Dakota Hogback in 1971, rock layers revealing 45 million years of geologic history were exposed. To see them, take I-70 west from Denver to Exit 259. Turn right at the bottom of the exit ramp and almost immediately turn right again to enter the T-Rex parking lot. A 0.21-mile paved path ascends gently to the northeast and has many informational signs about the geologic history of this area. Limestone, sandstone, and carbonaceous claystone layers are easily visible. Deposited between 140 and 95 million years ago when this region was under water, the layers reached the surface approximately 70 million years ago when the Rockies were uplifted. Because dinosaur fossil bones and footprints have been found here, this part of the Dakota Hogback is known as Dinosaur Ridge.

8. Dakota Hogback (Dinosaur Ridge) Trail

DEGREE OF DIFFICULTY: Moderate
ROUND-TRIP DISTANCE: 1.20 miles
ROUND-TRIP TIME: 75 minutes (45 minutes up, 30 minutes down)
STARTING ALTITUDE: 6,396 feet
ELEVATION GAINED: Approximately 200 feet
MAP: Matthews/Winters Park brochure

Getting There: From the junction of U.S. 285 with C-470, drive west on C-470 for 6.3 miles to I-70. Continue west for 1.1 miles to the Morrison exit (Exit 259). At the stoplight at the bottom of the exit ramp, turn left (south) onto Colorado Highway 26 for 0.3 mile and make the second left into the Stegosaurus parking lot. The trail begins at its south end at the Dinosaur Ridge Raptor Migration Station sign.

The Hike: The trail climbs for 55 feet before turning left to join a service road running up from the highway. The service road ascends moderately steeply northeast toward the ridge. At 0.05 mile, there is a gate; pass through the opening on the left. At 0.18 mile, the trail turns right just before a gate blocking access to a shooting range. The ascent is still steep and overlooks the busy and noisy I-70 and the quieter state highway.

Head south, keeping the shooting range on your left. The ascent is more gentle now, and the trail is wide. At 0.44 mile, look southwest to Red Rocks Park as you walk on the west side of the crest of the ridge. At 0.50 mile, the trail descends slightly and again ascends at 0.52 mile. It crosses under wires strung with large colored balls designed to discourage aircraft from flying too low up and down the valley. At 0.56 mile, there is a short path to the left that leads to several stone steps and a high point on the ridge. This is the raptor monitoring area. Continue south on the ridge as the trail winds in and out of the trees. You will reach the crest at 0.60 mile. Off to the east, Bear Creek Lake and the Soda Lakes can be seen, as well as the plains. Mt. Morrison (7,861 feet) and Red Rocks Park are off to the west. At this point, we suggest turning back and visiting the raptor station, if it is open.

9. Mt. Vernon Village Walk

DEGREE OF DIFFICULTY: Easy
ROUND-TRIP DISTANCE: 1.15 miles
ROUND-TRIP TIME: 40 minutes
STARTING ALTITUDE: 6,300 feet
ELEVATION GAIN: Approximately 200 feet
MAP: Matthews/Winters Park brochure

When you are ready for lunch or a rest, drive a short distance across Colorado Highway 26 to the Matthews/ Winters parking area, named for two of the people who sold or donated land to form the park in 1982. Picnic tables under the trees next to Mt. Vernon Creek make an excellent stopping point prior to taking this interesting walk.

Getting There: If driving directly from home, follow the directions to the Dakota Hogback (Dinosaur Ridge) Trail, but instead of turning left into the Stegosaurus parking lot, take the next right into the Matthews/Winters parking area. If coming from the Stegosaurus parking lot after taking the Dakota Hogback Trail, cross Colorado Highway 26, turn left (south), and almost immediately turn right into the Matthews/Winters parking lot. A flight of steps leads down to a signboard with an area map and historical information. A brochure box is nearby.

The Hike: The wide gravel trail initially heads southwest. At 0.04 mile, a path to the right leads to toilets. At 0.06 mile, pass picnic tables under willow and cottonwood trees along Mt. Vernon Creek. Cross the creek at 0.07 mile. The path soon forks, and we suggest going right. There is a gradual ascent into a wide meadow. The trail swings west at 0.13 mile. A private home sits off to the right, beyond which I-70 is visible. At 0.21 mile, the trail abruptly turns south.

Continue to ascend into the meadow, which is full of wildflowers in spring. Mt. Morrison (7,861 feet) is off to the right. At 0.36 mile, reach the crest of a hill. From here, enjoy fine views of the foothills to the southwest, as well as two sections of Dinosaur Ridge with a saddle between them off to the east.

At 0.37 mile, a 135-foot trail to the right leads to a small enclosed cemetery. Several wooden grave markers are still in place, but their faces are completely eroded. Two gravestones from 1860 and 1867 are still legible. Another nearby enclosure protects a grave site with a wooden cross devoid

of lettering. There is a great sense of peace here, with the wind sighing and the beautiful view of the land rising and falling away.

Regain the trail at 0.42 mile. At 0.48 mile, the Red Rocks Trail splits off to the right, but you take a left on the Village Trail, which curves around a ridge, parallels Highway 26, and heads north. Descend toward the wooded creek, reach the trees at 0.99 mile, and follow the creek to the fork just west of the footbridge at 1.08 miles. Turn right and return to the signboard at 1.15 miles, then continue to the parking lot.

The saddle on Dinosaur Ridge from Mt. Vernon Village Walk.

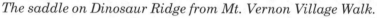

Lair O' The Bear Park

This 319-acre park, part of Jefferson County Open Space, opened in 1991. It has 4.3 miles of trails and encompasses nearly 1.5 miles of Bear Creek. The riparian zone ecosystem greatly increases the diversity of wildlife in this area. Not only are deer, elk, small mammals, and birds common to the foothills found here, but reptiles, beaver, amphibians, fish, and waterfowl as well. Particularly noteworthy along the creek banks is the American dipper, or water ouzel. The flora, too, is varied and includes cottonwood, alder, chokecherry, box elder, willow, blue spruce, Douglas fir, ponderosa pine, juniper, yucca, ferns, and mosses. Fishermen find rainbow and brown trout in the stream, and a handicapped-accessible fishing deck has been built out over the water, close to the parking area.

The two hikes described would be appropriate for conditioning early in the spring and are quite pleasant in the fall as well. The heat is intense in summer; we discourage their use at that time.

10. The Creekside Trail

DEGREE OF DIFFICULTY: Easy
ROUND-TRIP DISTANCE: 1.32 miles
ROUND-TRIP TIME: 45 minutes
STARTING ALTITUDE: 6,500 feet
ELEVATION GAIN: Approximately 50 feet
MAP: Lair O' The Bear Park brochure

Getting There: From the junction of U.S. 285 and C-470, head west on U.S. 285 South for 1.9 miles to the Evergreen–Morrison–Colorado Highway 8 exit. Turn right onto Colorado Highway 8 for 2.3 miles and turn left at a stoplight onto Colorado Highway 74 toward Evergreen. This turn at the western edge of Morrison avoids the town's often busy main street. The road winds up Bear Creek Canyon past Idledale. At 4.7 miles, turn left into the Lair O' The Bear parking lot, where there are restrooms, picnic tables and benches, and a water pump.

The Hike: At the start of the trail, there is a signboard with an area map and a box with park maps. Walk straight (south), past a trail on the left that leads to the picnic area, to a sign for the Creekside Trail at 0.06 mile. Turn left (downstream) and at 0.08 mile reach the handicapped fishing deck built out over the creek. Several paths lead off to

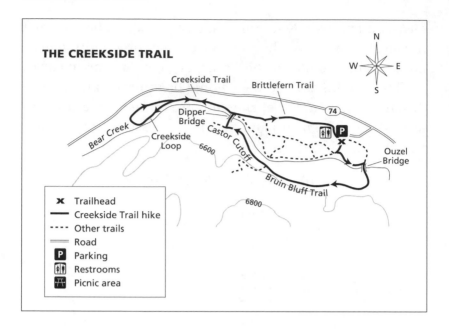

the left to picnic tables. Walk through an area of willows past a bench at 0.21 mile. The dirt trail is quite wide. At 0.29 mile, turn right onto the Brittlefern Trail and immediately cross the Ouzel Bridge, where there is a bench at 0.30 mile. Turn right onto the Bruin Bluff Trail and begin a gentle ascent through the trees. At 0.45 mile, there is a bench, and just beyond it is a fork in the trail. Head right, onto the Castor Cutoff. The trail descends gently. At 0.73 mile, turn right, back onto the Bruin Bluff Trail, which crosses the Dipper Bridge to a bench and joins the Creekside Trail. Turn left onto the Creekside Trail, and at 0.85 mile turn left again at a sign indicating the Creekside Loop Nature Walk. At 0.88 mile, there is another bench in a pretty area overlooking the creek, which is quite wide and fast.

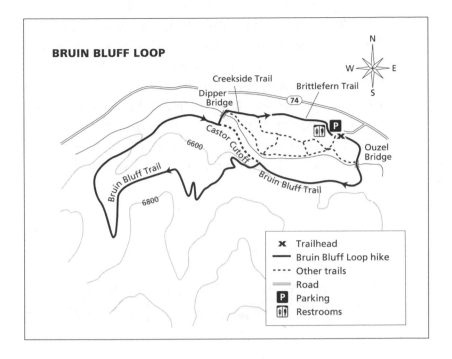

At 0.97 mile, the path loops back toward the Creekside Trail, rejoining it at 1.10 miles. At 1.21 miles, pass the Dipper Bridge. Continue straight back to the parking lot.

11. Bruin Bluff Loop

DEGREE OF DIFFICULTY: Easy
ROUND-TRIP DISTANCE: 1.58 miles
ROUND-TRIP TIME: 60 minutes
STARTING ALTITUDE: 6,500 feet
ELEVATION GAIN: Approximately 250 feet
MAP: Lair O' The Bear Park brochure

Getting There: The directions are the same as for the Creekside Trail (Hike #10).

The Hike: Follow directions for the Creekside Trail hike up to the Castor Cutoff. Instead of taking a right onto the cutoff, go left on the Bruin Bluff Trail. Ascend through conifers, gradually at first, and then more steeply. At 0.60 mile, the path becomes even steeper and rockier. At 0.63 and at 0.64 mile, switchbacks lead up and around a gully. Descend to a bench at 0.76 mile, then ascend through two more switchbacks to the high point of the hike at 0.91 mile. Gradually descend to a bench at 1.11 miles and the creek at 1.37 miles. At 1.44 miles, turn left at a fork, cross the Dipper Bridge to the Creekside Trail, and turn right to the parking lot.

Pine Valley Ranch Park

This gem of a park is well worth the drive time. The area, first homesteaded in 1896, was purchased by an ice company in 1908. Ice cut from man-made lakes formed by diverting water from the North Fork of the South Platte River was shipped to Denver via the narrow gauge Colorado and Southern Railroad. In 1925, William Baehr, a Chicago businessman, bought the property and erected a summer home in the style of Black Forest manor houses. A crew of 60 allegedly worked 24 hours a day to complete the project. Over time, an observatory, pagoda, ice shed, barn, waterwheel, and teahouse were added. The Pine Valley Ranch Depot, which sits nearby, was once a gardener's shed and fishing hut. By 1937, the railroad was abandoned, and in 1956 the property was purchased by a group of Denver residents for use as a fishing retreat. In 1975 an Iowa corporation bought the property and added more buildings and amenities, advertising it as a conference and retreat center as well as resort. Jefferson County Open Space bought the lodge and the surrounding 820 acres in 1986 for $2.35 million and developed the current 770-acre park. The lodge is under restoration, but its future use has not been disclosed.

After the gold rush of 1859, settlers followed the North Fork of the South Platte River into the mountains. The nearby town of Pine was established in 1872 and thrived on logging. The community boomed after the narrow gauge railroad from Denver to Pine was completed in 1878. As many as 11 sawmills were active in the area, producing railroad ties and lumber for local use and Denver construction. Most of the original forest was cut and harvested, leaving only stunted and malformed trees. The area gradually became barren, wildlife moved to better habitats, and much of the area's scenic and commercial quality diminished.

12. The Narrow Gauge Trail, the North Fork View Trail, and the Pine Lake Loop

DEGREE OF DIFFICULTY: Easy
ROUND-TRIP DISTANCE: 3.71 miles
ROUND-TRIP TIME: 1 hour 45 minutes
STARTING ALTITUDE: Approximately 6,900 feet
ELEVATION GAIN: Approximately 250 feet
MAP: Pine Valley Ranch Park brochure

Getting There: From the intersection of U.S. 285 and C-470, drive 21.8 miles west on U.S. 285 South through Conifer to the stoplight at Pine Junction. Turn left onto Jefferson County Road 126 (South Pine Valley Road) and

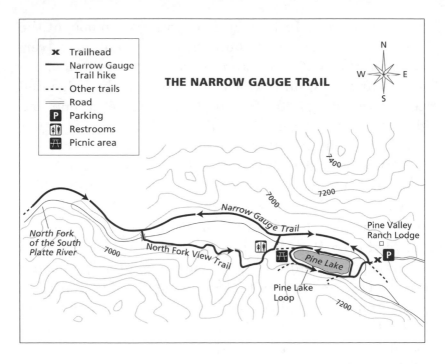

descend about 1,500 feet in 6.2 miles on a winding paved road to a sharp right turn onto Crystal Lake Road. Drive 0.6 mile to enter the park. There are three parking lots; if possible, go to the lowest one, which is closest to the North Fork of the South Platte River. At the west end of the lot, there are well-kept restrooms and a drinking fountain. Covered picnic tables with a fireplace and grills are below the lot, next to the river.

The Hike: We have combined three short hikes into one longer one. Begin walking on a wide paved path to the right of the restrooms, heading down to the river. At 0.02 mile, there is an information signboard and a box of park maps. At 0.03 mile, take the Narrow Gauge Trail, leading off to the right. This wide dirt path, on which horses and bikers are permitted, runs upstream adjacent to the noisy, fast river. You are now on the old bed of the narrow gauge railroad. There are many willows between you and the river, and beyond that is a meadow sloping up to conifer-covered hillsides. The ascent is gentle. At 0.35 mile, the North Fork View Trail veers left over a bridge. Stay straight and at 0.43 mile pass an old diversion dam on the left.

One appeal of this hike is that the river is often in full view. At 0.77 mile, the North Fork View Trail comes back in from the left. Continue straight up the narrowing valley. At 0.97 mile, the valley widens again. The trail now curves south along the park boundary fence. At 1.28 miles, you walk right next to the river. The trail ends at a gate at the Open Space boundary at 1.45 miles, beyond which is private property.

Turn around, and gradually descend back to the North Fork View Trail at 2.12 miles. Go right over the bridge. This narrow, dirt-and-grass trail is for hikers only and cuts across the meadow. The trail curves toward the river, which you will reach at 2.51 miles. Restrooms and a covered picnic area are located to the right. Cross a bridge at 2.58 miles to the Narrow Gauge Trail and turn right, back to the starting point at 2.93 miles. Nearby is the Pine Valley Ranch Depot, with picnic tables and an information center open from 12 to 4 P.M. on weekends.

At the starting point, there is a sign for the Pine Lake Loop. Cross a bridge, go left on a paved walk, and pass steps leading steeply up the hillside. This is the Park View Trail, which we omitted because it gains 430 feet in only 0.8 mile. Reach the lake at 0.11 mile and go right around it

The South Platte River, Pine Valley Ranch Park.

on a wide dirt trail. There are three wooden observation decks built out over the water.

Continue walking west, with the lake on your left and the river on your right. There is a beaver dam at the west end, and just beyond it at 0.40 mile are restrooms and a covered picnic area.

The trail now curves east. A bench is located at 0.44 mile, just beyond the Buck Gulch Trail, which goes off to the right. There is another bench at 0.52 mile. Continue back to the starting point at 0.75 mile.

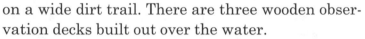

Apex Park

Apex Park has grown to 661 acres, with 8.3 miles of trails. The trailhead shares parking with the Heritage

Square Shopping Center (the site of Apex City) above Golden. Though the hikes here are interesting and varied, the park suffers by comparison with other Jefferson County Open Space parks because there are no benches or toilet facilities on its eastern end.

Founded during the gold rush that followed John Gregory's 1859 strike in the Central City area, Apex City served as the eastern terminus of the Apex and Gregory Gulch Wagon Toll Road. Two competing routes to the Gregory Diggings were the Golden Gate Canyon Road and the Mt. Vernon Canyon Road. The Apex and Gregory Gulch wagon road was profitable until floods wiped out most of the toll roads in 1878–1879. In 1880, the Jefferson County commissioners bought and repaired the Mt. Vernon Canyon Road and declared it a public right-of-way, causing the Apex and Gregory Gulch wagon road to fall into disuse.

13. The Apex Trail Loop

DEGREE OF DIFFICULTY: Moderate
ROUND-TRIP DISTANCE: 4.13 miles
ROUND-TRIP TIME: 2 hours 45 minutes
STARTING ALTITUDE: Approximately 6,200 feet
ELEVATION GAIN: Approximately 1,000 feet
MAP: Apex Park brochure

Getting There: Drive west on C-470 from its junction with U.S. 285 for 6.3 miles to I-70. Take I-70 west for 1.1 miles and turn off at the Morrison exit (Exit 259). At the stoplight at the bottom of the exit ramp, turn right to U.S. 40 and immediately turn right (east) again. At 0.9 mile, turn left into the large Heritage Square Shopping Center parking lot. The trailhead is near the southeast end of the lot.

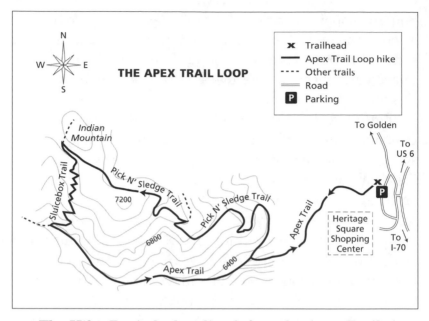

The Hike: Begin by heading left at the Apex Trail sign. After 80 feet, cross a bridge over a gully. Turn left onto the dirt-and-gravel trail at 0.04 mile and ascend westward gradually into Apex Gulch. Heritage Square is to the left; a housing subdivision is to the right. Continue southwest into the gulch, keeping an eye out for bikers. The trail rises and dips as it climbs. Apex Creek is to the left. At 0.45 mile, you will pass a Jeffco Rules and Regulations sign, and at 0.47 mile, a difficult-to-read signboard map. The trail is intermittently rocky.

At 0.59 mile, turn right onto the Pick N' Sledge Trail, which ascends along the exposed and hot east face of a hill. Small shrubs and yucca dot the area. On a hill to the right is a ski tow. Ahead, there is a fine view of Denver and the eastern plains. The Table Mountains, with Golden lying at their base, are visible to the north.

Table Mountain from the Apex Trail Loop.

The trail switchbacks at 0.82 and 0.98 mile, and the ascent becomes steeper. Wildflowers are usually blooming along the route. There is another switchback at 1.18 miles. Ponderosa pines grow at 1.43 miles, and the trail switchbacks again at 1.47 miles. Enjoy the good views to the northeast. At 1.53 miles, reach the Grubstake Loop junction but stay left on the Pick N' Sledge Trail, which climbs toward Indian Mountain. The trail is now narrow and rocky through an evergreen forest.

Switchback again at 1.65 miles. The trail then ascends to a meadow at 1.87 miles. The Jefferson County Courthouse is visible to the right. At 1.97 miles, reach the trail crest. Houses are visible on adjacent hills.

Head left on the Sluicebox Trail at 2.11 miles and ignore the Grubstake Trail to the right. Between 2.22 and

2.75 miles, there are 12 switchbacks leading down to the Apex Trail, which you will reach at 2.79 miles. The trail now descends through Apex Gulch, with the creek on the right. Cottonwoods flourish in places, as do scrub brush and wildflowers. The trail drops more steeply at 3.41 miles. Arrive at the junction with the Pick N' Sledge Trail at 3.54 miles. Descend to the trailhead.

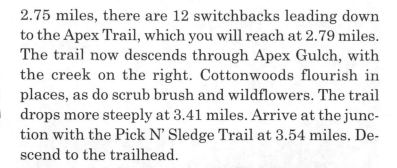

Mt. Falcon Park

The history of this area is integrally connected with that of John B. Walker, who owned 4,000 acres of land here at the beginning of the twentieth century. A West Point dropout, he eventually earned a Ph.D. from Georgetown University and even served in the Chinese army. Walker became wealthy from land speculation in West Virginia and at one time owned *Cosmopolitan* magazine and the Stanley Steamer Company. He sold the Red Rocks Park area to the City of Denver. His dream was to build a summer residence for U.S. presidents on a ridge near his home, erected in 1909 on 7,851-foot Mt. Falcon. A fund drive collected $.10 apiece from thousands of Colorado schoolchildren, and the foundation cornerstone was laid in 1911, but financial reverses soon put a stop to Walker's pipe dream. In 1918, Walker's home was struck by lightning and burned, leaving only the stone ruins visible today. He died in poverty in 1931 at age 83.

Mt. Falcon Park is part of Jefferson County Open Space.

14. The Castle Trail

DEGREE OF DIFFICULTY: Easy
ROUND-TRIP DISTANCE: 3.60 miles
ROUND-TRIP TIME: 2 hours
STARTING ALTITUDE: 7,400 feet (upper parking lot)
ELEVATION GAIN: 213 feet (Summer White House)
MAPS: Mount Falcon Park brochure, USGS Morrison

This trail is popular with hikers and bikers. No water is available along the way, so carry plenty with you, as temperatures are quite hot in summer. The trail rises and falls, making it difficult to calculate elevation gained and lost.

Getting There: Although you can enter the park from the east via Colorado Highway 8 south of Morrison, we prefer the west entrance because it is closer to the trails we describe. From Denver, drive west on U.S. 285 South (which starts out as Hampden Avenue) to its junction with C-470. From there, continue on U.S. 285 South for 4.4 miles and make a right turn onto Parmalee Gulch Road, which is preceded by a sign for Mt. Falcon Park. This paved road winds upward for 2.8 miles, where another Mt. Falcon Park sign directs you to turn right onto the unpaved Picutis Road.

At this point, the road signage gets confusing. Fortunately, there are a number of clearly visible park signs to direct you. A few feet after you turn onto Picutis Road, turn left onto Comanche Road for 0.1 mile, at which point you turn right onto OhKay Road, which ascends for 0.1 mile to another right turn back onto Picutis Road. The winding ascent continues.

After another 0.5 mile, bear left on Picutis Road where Nambe Road joins it on the right. You will find a surprising sign 0.6 mile farther down the road, indicating that you

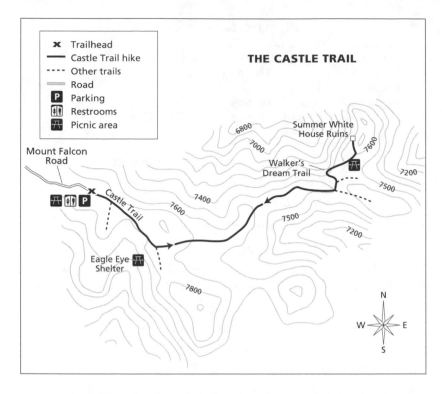

are now on Nambe Road. A few feet beyond this is a sign on the left, stating that you are now on Mt. Falcon Road! After an additional 0.6 mile, you enter the park at the lower parking lot used only for horse trailers and buses. Continue for 0.1 more mile to the upper parking lot (2.0 miles from where you turned initially onto Picutis Road). Picnic areas are located above and below this lot.

The Hike: Take the dirt road marked by a Castle Trail sign at the east end of the parking lot. At 0.05 mile, there is a signboard with a map. Park brochures are available here. At 0.10 mile, a sign indicates the Castle Trail straight ahead (the Parmalee Trail goes to the right). Restrooms are just beyond. The trail descends through conifers and provides a good view into the valley to the southeast. A bench is located at 0.23 mile. The trail now ascends through an area of burned-out trees to a fork at 0.38 mile. The Castle Trail continues to the left; the Meadow Trail and the path to the Eagle Eye Shelter go right.

Remain on the Castle Trail and continue your gradual ascent. At the top of the hill (0.44 mile), there is a good view of Bear Lake to the east. The trail now descends, gradually at first, but then more steeply. Another bench is located at 0.54 mile. A meadow off to the right is full of wildflowers in the spring. At 0.79 mile, arrive at another fork. Turn left to reach the fenced-off Walker Home ruins in 0.04 mile. Benches and an informative poster are situated here.

Return to the Castle Trail, continue east past the Meadow Trail, and descend through conifers and scrub oak. You come to another bench at 1.13 miles, and soon you can see Red Rocks Amphitheater to the northeast. At 1.29 miles, pass the Two-Dog Trail on your right.

Continue on the Castle Trail, which now offers beautiful views of the Front Range to the northeast. At 1.38 miles, a sign marks a trail to the left that leads to Walker's Dream. Before taking it, spend a little time in a roofed picnic area just beyond, from which you can see Bear Lake and the Denver skyline to the east. The 0.41-mile trail to the ruins of the Summer White House at 7,613 feet is steep and rocky, but there are excellent views to the east as you ascend. Note the bench 0.27 mile up the trail. From here, you can see all the way from Mt. Evans to Longs Peak. At a fork in the trail at 0.34 mile, an additional path leads to a scenic view point overlooking Red Rocks Amphitheater and the Dakota Hogback. Back on the trail, you reach the ruins almost immediately, at 1.80 miles from your start. There is a poster with sketches of the proposed Summer White House and pictures of the laying of the granite cornerstone. A sign states that this was a gift of the people of Colorado in 1911.

Retrace your steps to the parking lot.

15. Eagle Eye Shelter and the Tower Trail

DEGREE OF DIFFICULTY: Easy
ROUND-TRIP DISTANCE: 2.44 miles
ROUND-TRIP TIME: 1 hour 15 minutes
STARTING ALTITUDE: 7,400 feet (upper parking lot)
ELEVATION GAIN: 450 feet (at the tower)
MAPS: Mt. Falcon Park brochure, USGS Morrison

Getting There: Follow directions to the upper Mt. Falcon parking lot given for the Castle Trail (Hike #14).

The Hike: This hike consists of a loop off the Castle Trail. It is easier to go to the Eagle Eye Shelter first, then to the tower, and then on a gradual descent back to the Castle Trail, rather than making a long ascent to the tower.

At first, the directions are the same as for the Castle Trail. Take the dirt road marked by a Castle Trail sign at the east end of the parking lot. At 0.05 mile you will come to the signboard with the area map. At 0.10 mile, a sign indicates the Castle Trail straight ahead. Take this to the fork at 0.38 mile. Instead of bearing left on the Castle Trail, take the right fork for the Meadow Trail and the Eagle Eye Shelter. Just beyond the trail signs is a two-sided covered bench off to the right.

The trail descends slightly to another bench at 0.46 mile. At the beginning of a moderately steep ascent, signs direct

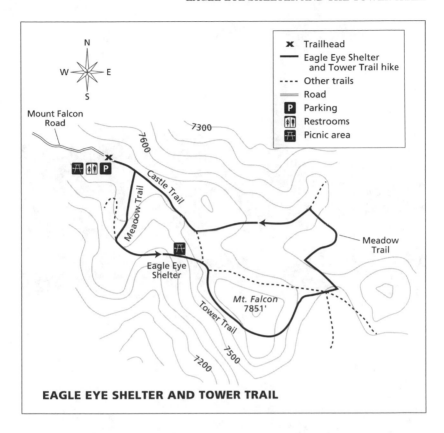

EAGLE EYE SHELTER AND TOWER TRAIL

you straight ahead to the Eagle Eye Shelter and the Tower Trail (the Meadow Trail goes off to the left). At 0.60 mile, reach the shelter entrance. A sign notes that this was a family cabin from 1933 to 1972. The 100-foot path to the shelter is paved with marble chips, and the structure itself contains four large picnic tables and benches. Immediately adjacent is an overlook with excellent views of Mt. Evans, other Front Range peaks, and the highway.

Leaving the cabin, follow the Tower Trail up several flights of steps to the tower itself, located at 0.79 mile. Climb 14 wooden steps to the covered viewing platform, where

Walker home ruins, Mt. Falcon Park.

Mt. Evans from the Eagle Eye Shelter, Mt. Falcon Park.

there is a bench. A panoramic view of the peaks to the west and the plains to the east awaits you.

When you leave the tower, turn left onto the trail, and at 0.81 mile pass a sign indicating a horse trail to the right. There is a small corral to your left. Just beyond, there is a poorly marked 110-foot trail to the right that will take you up to the edge of a cliff if you wish. The views here are not as good as those you have already seen. Continue your descent across the eastern face of the mountain and down several steep switchbacks, arriving at a three-way trail junction at 1.23 miles, where there is another bench. The Parmalee Trail heads off to the right, but you continue to the left on the Meadow Trail for about 400 feet to another fork. Take the left fork, remaining on the Meadow Trail (the Old Ute Trail goes to the right).

At 1.46 miles, cross a small bridge over a creek and continue your descent on the winding path. The Meadow Trail then gradually climbs through conifers to its junction with the Castle Trail at 1.66 miles. Turn left onto the Castle Trail and follow it back to the parking lot.

White Ranch Park

Ute and Arapaho are thought to have hunted and camped here centuries ago. Permanent settlers first took up residence in 1865. In the early 1900s, the land was homesteaded by the White family, who began a cattle operation that lasted from 1913 until 1969. White Ranch Park was created in 1975 out of several land purchases and a gift of land from the family. It has grown to 4,207 acres with 19.7 miles of trails. The views of the high plains to the east, once dotted with buffalo, are entrancing. The park forms part of Jefferson County Open Space.

16. Rawhide, Longhorn, Maverick, and Sawmill Trails Loop

DEGREE OF DIFFICULTY: Easy
ROUND-TRIP DISTANCE: 2.44 miles
ROUND-TRIP TIME: 1 hour 30 minutes
STARTING ALTITUDE: 7,500 feet
ELEVATION GAIN: Approximately 300 feet
MAP: White Ranch Park brochure

Getting There: From its junction with Wadsworth Boulevard, go west on 6th Avenue (U.S. 6) for 9.7 miles to its merger with Colorado Highway 93. Proceed 1.4 miles and make a left turn onto Golden Gate Canyon Road. Drive for 4.1 miles and turn right at Crawford Gulch Road. Continue for another 4.1 miles and make a right turn onto Belcher Hill Road. Drive 1.8 more miles, much of it on a dirt road, past the first parking lot to the second and lower one, the main west parking area. A signboard with an area map, park brochures, and warnings about bear and mountain lions are located here. Picnic tables and benches are nearby. A 0.17-mile trail to more picnic facilities and toilets features exhibits of various farm implements, such as a sulky plow, a disc and a spike harrow, a seed drill, and a haymow.

The Hike: From the northeast side of the parking lot, begin hiking on the Rawhide Trail. The path is slightly rocky and somewhat narrow as it descends gently through a meadow. Pass two benches and a memorial plaque on the

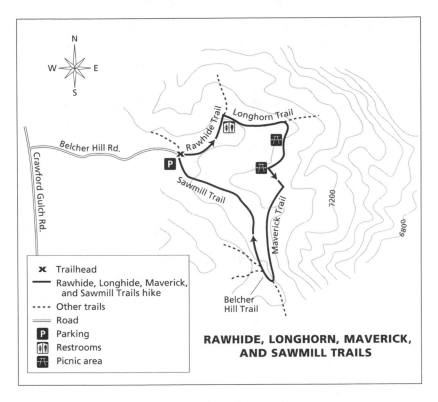

RAWHIDE, LONGHORN, MAVERICK, AND SAWMILL TRAILS

Legend:
- ✘ Trailhead
- —— Rawhide, Longhide, Maverick, and Sawmill Trails hike
- ---- Other trails
- ═══ Road
- 🅿 Parking
- 🚻 Restrooms
- ⛾ Picnic area

left. Enjoy fine views of the surrounding hills as you descend. The trail curves east. At 0.24 mile, go right on the Longhorn Trail. Pass among widely spaced ponderosa pines, which allow good views of the Great Plains to the northeast. At 0.44 mile, an unmarked trail comes in from the right to join the Longhorn Trail.

The descent is now a bit steeper and rockier. At 0.51 mile, the Table Mountains are visible to the east. You encounter a switchback at 0.68 mile. At 0.73 mile, take the Maverick Trail to the right. You are now heading southeast, with a steep drop to your left. The trail curves into a gully, crosses a small meadow, and descends to the creekbed, often dry in late summer. Now ascend through the pines. Arrive at the crest of a hill at 1.20 miles, and another one at 1.37 miles. Again there are good views to the east. Reach a final crest at 1.65 miles. Turn right onto the Belcher Hill Trail, which is actually an old road, at 1.70 miles. At 1.79 miles, turn right onto the Sawmill Trail, another old road, which descends past a beautiful hay field. Bear left on this trail at a fork and pass a group of ranch buildings. The trail soon ascends to the parking lot.

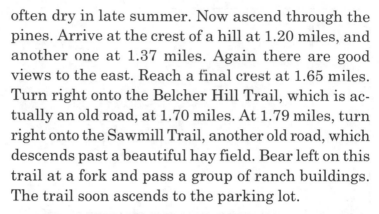

Lookout Mountain Nature Center and Preserve

Charles Boettcher built a summerhouse, now called a mansion, on Lookout Mountain in 1917. In 1968, the home and 110 acres were donated to Jefferson County. The new nature center, a lovely facility, opened in 1997. Many of its structural components are made from recycled materials—for example, floor tiles from windshields. There are 1.4 miles of trails for hikers only, marred only by the presence of many radio and television transmitters near the preserve.

The nature center is open from 10:00 A.M. to 4:00 P.M. on Tuesday through Friday, and from 10:00 A.M. to 6:00 P.M. on weekends. It contains beautiful displays of wildlife, flora, and carved birds that hang from the ceiling. Recorded sounds of birds and insects complement the displays. Binoculars are available for meadow viewing, and Pikes Peak is visible on a clear day. Tee shirts, costume jewelry, and a small selection of books are available for purchase.

17. The Nature Trail

DEGREE OF DIFFICULTY: Easy
ROUND-TRIP DISTANCE: 1.21 miles
ROUND-TRIP TIME: 40 minutes
STARTING ALTITUDE: 7,540 feet
ELEVATION GAIN: 120 feet
MAP: Lookout Mountain Nature Center and Preserve brochure

Getting There: From the junction of U.S. 285 with C-470, go west on C-470 for 6.3 miles and exit onto I-70 westbound. Turn off at the Lookout Mountain exit (Exit 256). At the off-ramp stop sign, turn right and make an immediate left onto U.S. 40 going to Lookout Mountain. At 1.5 miles, turn right onto Lookout Mountain Road. Drive another 1.5 miles and make a left turn onto Colorow Road. After 1.2 more miles, make a sharp right turn into the parking area for the nature center and the Boettcher Mansion.

The Hike: Start at the Nature Trail sign just east of the mansion. At 75 feet, ignore the trail on the left that goes to the nature center; stay right as the trail descends through evergreens. At 0.04 mile, go left at the Forest Loop Trail sign. The trail descends and winds across a meadow of native grasses, wildflowers, and widely spaced evergreens. The dirt-and-gravel trail is wide and easy. There is a bench at 0.17 mile. At 0.20 mile, cross a small wooden bridge over a dry creekbed. When you come to a fork at 0.24 mile, take the Meadow Loop Trail to the left. This trail continues to descend, then curves around the base of the meadow. To the left (east), Denver and the plains are visible.

Now begin your ascent, gradually heading north. At 0.72 mile, traverse a small aspen grove. A bench is located at 0.74 mile. At 0.76 mile, note the old stone chimney to the

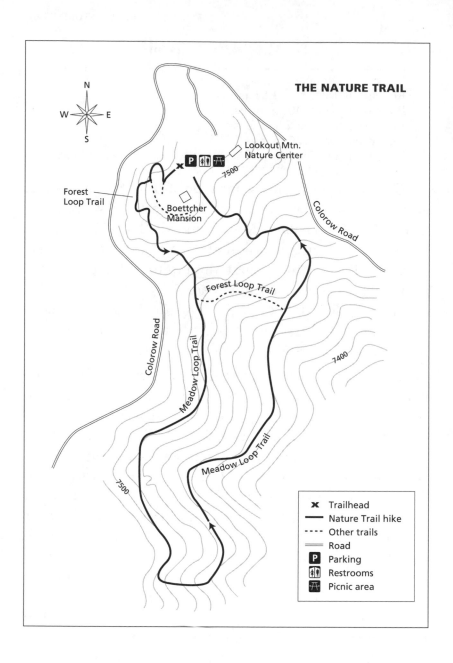

THE NATURE TRAIL

N
W · E
S

Lookout Mtn.
Nature Center

P · 7500

Forest
Loop Trail

Boettcher
Mansion

Colorow Road

Forest Loop Trail

Colorow Road

Meadow Loop Trail

7400

Meadow Loop Trail

7500

✖	Trailhead
—	Nature Trail hike
----	Other trails
═	Road
P	Parking
🛉🛉	Restrooms
⛫	Picnic area

left before encountering another bench at 0.98 mile. Intersect the Forest Loop Trail at 0.99 mile, turn left (north), and cross a small bridge at 1.00 mile. At 1.05 miles, a sign on the right points to the nature center. At 1.12 miles, turn left and pass a kiosk on the right. At 1.15 miles, turn right and walk to the nature center on a built-up trail, passing a signboard on the left. You reach the center at 1.21 miles.

Alderfer/Three Sisters Park

This 770-acre park is named for a ranching family who donated a portion of the land and for the outcropping of metamorphic rock (primarily quartz) called the Three Sisters. Another similar high, rocky point is called the Brother. Many different species of birds and small mammals reside in the park's pine forests. The park, which is part of Jefferson County Open Space, offers two fine hikes.

18. The Three Sisters and the Brother Trail

DEGREE OF DIFFICULTY: Moderate
ROUND-TRIP DISTANCE: 3.32 miles
ROUND-TRIP TIME: 2 hours 30 minutes
STARTING ALTITUDE: 7,600 feet
ELEVATION GAIN: Approximately 210 feet
MAP: Alderfer/Three Sisters Park brochure

Getting There: From the junction of U.S. 285 and C-470, go west on U.S. 285 South for 1.9 miles to the Evergreen–Morrison–Colorado Highway 8 exit. Turn right onto Colorado Highway 8 for 2.3 miles and turn left at a stoplight onto Colorado Highway

74 toward Evergreen. This turn at the western edge of Morrison avoids the town's often busy main street. Take Highway 74 for 8.8 miles through Bear Creek Canyon past Idledale and Kittredge to the first stoplight in Evergreen. Turn left onto Colorado Highway 73, travel 0.6 mile, and veer to the right onto winding Buffalo Park Road. Pass the Evergreen High School on your left, and at 1.4 miles, pass the lower (east) lot for the park on the right. Continue 0.9 mile more to the west parking area and turn right. You will have traveled 15.9 miles from the U.S. 285/C-470 junction.

The Hike: The directions given for this hike in four different trail guides frequently confused us. After attempting it several ways, we believe that our modifications are now accurate and more suitable for seniors. Though the hike's length and altitude are not great, we believe that the steepness of some of the ascents warrants a difficulty designation of moderate.

Start at the east end of the parking lot, near some portable toilets and a bench, where there is a signboard with an area map and a box of park brochures. Go left at the sign for the Bluebird Meadow Trail. Follow it northwest, parallel to the parking lot. Evergreen Mountain is to your left. At the west side of the lot, the trail heads north, then curves east through a lovely meadow. We chose to start the hike this way because it offers the best view of the Three Sisters ahead of you.

At 0.08 mile, turn right onto the Homestead Trail and continue east. In places, the dirt trail is built up over wetlands. At the top of the meadow, the trail curves south and at 0.41 mile intersects the Silver Fox Trail. Turn left onto the Silver Fox Trail and at 0.51 mile, where the Homestead

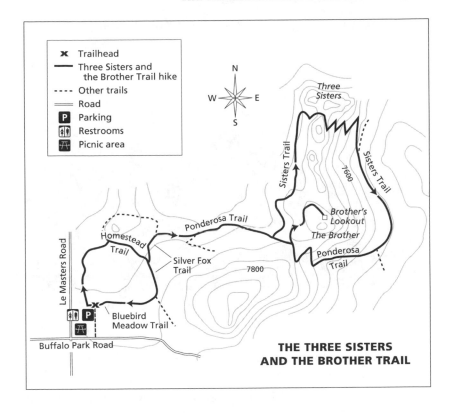

THE THREE SISTERS AND THE BROTHER TRAIL

Trail again comes in from the left, continue to the right on the Silver Fox. You now can take a good look at the Three Sisters. At 0.63 mile, ascend into the conifers, then go left on the Ponderosa Trail, which gently ascends and descends.

At 0.75 mile, the Sisters Trail angles off to the left. Our suggestion is to climb to the Brother Lookout first, while you are still fresh, rather than doing it near the end of the hike, when you may be hot and tired. Accordingly, head straight on the Ponderosa Trail to the Brother Lookout Trail at 0.82 mile. Turn left onto this moderately steep, rocky, and winding ascent and at 1.03 miles reach its end,

The Three Sisters, Alderfer/Three Sisters Park.

where you can look down at the high school. If you want a 360-degree panoramic view, carefully climb up the rocks to the southwest for about 30–40 feet to two stunted trees adjacent to the USGS benchmark. You can see the Three Sisters and Bergen Park to the northwest, Mt. Morrison to the northeast, Evergreen Mountain and Mt. Evans to the southwest, and Squaw Mountain to the northwest. Descend with care from the rocks.

Go back down to the Ponderosa Trail, turn right, and return to the Sisters Trail junction at 1.31 miles. Turn right onto it, and descend and ascend as it meanders around the base of the Three Sisters in a conifer forest. The wide spacing of the trees here allows good views. At 1.69 miles, the trail climbs over a saddle between the two northernmost Sisters. The ascent is now rather steep up several switchbacks. At 1.82 miles, reach the crest, where a sign on a tree to the left honors a cross-country runner from the high school. Descend via several steep switchbacks, enjoying a good view of Evergreen Lake from the first one. This is likely to be the hottest part of the hike.

At 2.15 miles, reach a junction with the Hidden Fawn Trail. Continue to the right on the Sisters Trail. Ascend gradually, and at 2.42 miles reach the intersection with the Ponderosa Trail. The Sisters Trail bears left, descending to the lower (east) parking lot, but you head straight, on the Ponderosa Trail. This ascends gradually at first and then more steeply, passing the trail to the Brother Lookout at 2.69 miles before descending gently to the intersection with the Silver Fox Trail at 2.88 miles. Turn right on Silver Fox, descend gradually, and when you break out of the trees, enjoy a good view of Mt. Evans ahead to the west.

At 3.00 and at 3.10 miles, ignore the Homestead Trail, which comes in from the right. At 3.11 miles, there is a bench. At 3.18 miles, turn right onto the Bluebird Meadow Trail and head back to your starting point at the parking lot.

19. Evergreen Mountain

DEGREE OF DIFFICULTY: Easy
ROUND-TRIP DISTANCE: 4.56 miles
ROUND-TRIP TIME: 3 hours
STARTING ALTITUDE: 7,600 feet
ELEVATION GAIN: 936 feet
MAP: Alderfer/Three Sisters Park brochure

Getting There: The directions are the same as for the Three Sisters and the Brother Trail (Hike #18).

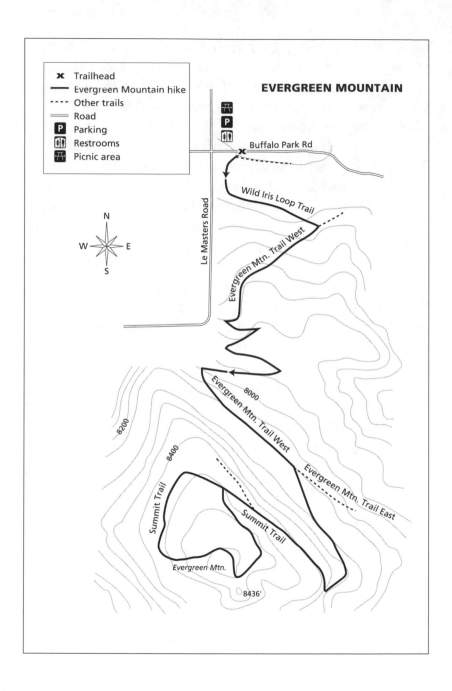

Evergreen Mountain, Alderfer / Three Sisters Park.

The Hike: From the southeast end of the parking lot, cross Buffalo Park Road to the start of the Wild Iris Loop Trail. Turn right and walk on the raised trail across a marshy area. At 0.28 mile, turn right at the sign indicating the Wild Iris Trail. At 0.30 mile, there is a bench, and a sign for the Evergreen Mountain Trail West. Take this wide trail through conifers and ascend several switchbacks. At 0.76 mile, a sign notes that the lodgepole pines have been thinned to strengthen the trees against attack by insects and disease.

At 1.29 miles, arrive at a junction with the Evergreen Mountain Trail East. Turn right and ascend the Summit Trail (which begins at this point), initially heading southeast. At 1.59 miles, it affords views of the valley and foothills. At 1.92 miles, a sign indicates a scenic view point to the right. At 1.95 miles, reach the Summit Loop. Go right and admire the peaks to the west. At 2.13 miles, an overlook provides a fine view of Mt. Evans. At 2.20 miles, reach the summit (8,536 feet) and enjoy more scenic views. When ready, retrace your steps to the parking lot.

Meyer Ranch Park

This 397-acre park with 3.8 miles of trails offers a contrast to some of the other areas we describe. Unlike high mountain terrain that offers hikers pristine lakes and stunning vistas, this park features aspen groves, lodgepole forest, and meadows of wildflowers in the spring. Deer and elk reside here. The trees have been thinned enough to allow plenty of sunshine to dapple the trails, and there is no feeling of being hemmed in.

The land was homesteaded in 1870 as a hay, lumber, and cattle ranch. It allegedly also served as winter animal quarters for the P. T. Barnum Circus in the late 1880s. A portion of the park was used in the 1940s for a ski hill. The Meyer family purchased the ranch in 1950, and in 1986 it was acquired by Jefferson County Open Space. The Colorado Department of Transportation is pursuing a wetlands restoration project here to clean water by filtration, decrease chances of flooding downstream, preserve animal habitat, and develop recreational activities.

The trails offer two loops—one easy and one moderately difficult. They make excellent conditioning hikes.

20. The Lodge Pole Loop

DEGREE OF DIFFICULTY: Easy
ROUND-TRIP DISTANCE: 1.97 miles
ROUND-TRIP TIME: 1 hour 5 minutes
STARTING ALTITUDE: 7,875 feet
ELEVATION GAIN: 361 feet
MAP: Meyer Ranch Park brochure

Getting There: From the junction of C-470 and U.S. 285, head west on U.S. 285 South. Turn right on South Turkey Creek Road, marked by a Meyer Ranch Open Space sign, at 11.7 miles. Continue for 0.2 mile, passing under the highway, to a stop sign, turn right, and immediately turn left into the parking area.

The Hike: From the parking lot, head south on a wide dirt-and-gravel road for 0.05 mile to a signboard with an area map and an adjacent brochure box. The trail heads west, then curves south at 0.12 mile. At 0.21 mile, there are toilets and a bench. The trail angles off to the right (southwest) and passes a log bench at 0.22 mile. Reach the Owl's Perch Trail at 0.24 mile. Go right into the lodgepole forest.

The trail curves around a large picnic area on the left, passes a bench at 0.27 mile, and reaches the Lodge Pole Loop at 0.41 mile. Go 20 feet to the left and turn right (south) on the Lodge Pole Loop straight up into the trees. The trail ascends southeast initially, then southwest, switchbacking at 0.49 mile, 0.52 mile, and 0.55 mile. At 0.58 mile, reach a sign indicating the Sunny Aspen Loop to the left. Continue on the Lodge Pole Loop to the right.

You will catch occasional glimpses of the neighboring hills through the trees. Follow gentle descents and ascents

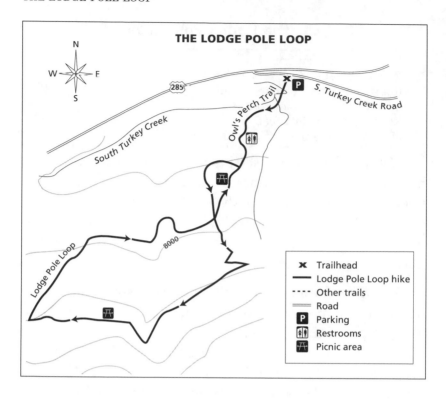

until you reach a bench and a small meadow at 0.79 mile. Cross a small footbridge at 0.94 mile over a gully and small stream where columbine bloom in the spring. Ascend gently under aspen trees, passing the Sunny Aspen Trail again on your left at 0.95 mile. Stay right on the Lodge Pole Loop.

Descend to the northwest and at 1.08 miles switchback northeast. Cross under power lines at 1.29 miles and note a covered bench to the left at 1.49 miles. The trail winds up and to the right before entering an open meadow and then an aspen grove. At 1.53 miles, an old road comes in from the right. Continue left into a meadow, where you can see the highway and mountaintops. Reach a sign for the Lodge

Pole Loop at 1.61 miles and pass a bench at 1.63 miles, just before the point where you started the loop.

Turn left down the Owl's Perch Trail, descend more steeply through the picnic area, and pass an old-fashioned water pump at 1.73 miles. Continue to retrace your steps to the parking lot.

21. Sunny Aspen Loop

DEGREE OF DIFFICULTY: Moderate
ROUND-TRIP DISTANCE: 2.38 miles
ROUND-TRIP TIME: 1 hour 54 minutes
STARTING ALTITUDE: 7,875 feet
ELEVATION GAIN: 465 feet
MAP: Meyer Ranch Park brochure

Longer and somewhat more difficult than the Lodge Pole Loop, this trail incorporates much of that hike. Its high point is 8,340 feet, making it a good conditioning hike for higher ascents. The combination of lodgepole pine and aspen with sunlight filtering through their branches makes for a most pleasant hike.

Getting There: The directions are the same as for the Lodge Pole Loop (Hike #20).

The Hike: From the parking lot, walk south 0.05 mile to a signboard with an area map and adjacent brochure box. Ascend gently on a wide dirt trail with a hay field to the right. Toilets and a bench are located at 0.21 mile, where the trail turns right and climbs to a picnic area. Pass a log bench at 0.22 mile, and at 0.24 mile reach a sign for the Owl's Perch Trail. Go left past an old-fashioned water pump, and at 0.35 mile reach the Lodge Pole Loop Trail, where there is another bench.

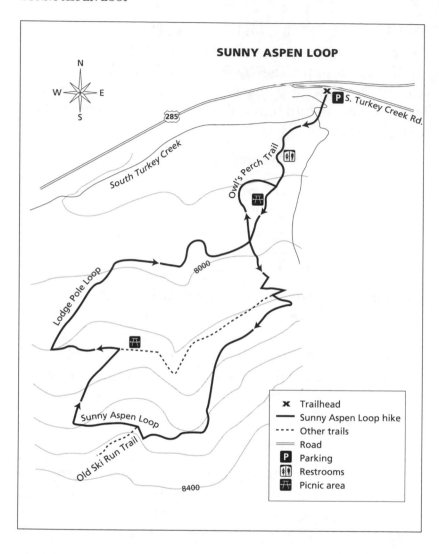

Climb straight ahead through aspen and into pines. Switchback to the south at 0.42 mile on an easy, wide trail. Switchback again at 0.45 mile and 0.49 mile. At 0.51 mile, go left (northeast) on the Sunny Aspen Trail, which is steeper and somewhat rocky. Switchback to the south at 0.56 mile, and soon the ascent gets steeper. Ignore a trail coming in from the left at 0.66 mile and continue straight before veering a bit to the right. At 0.73 mile, the trail angles left, and at 0.76 mile it curves toward the east. A trail sign at 0.80 mile indicates a jog to the left on a steeper, rockier slope. Ascending gradually, arrive at a stone picnic shelter and bench at 1.04 miles. The Old Ski Run Trail is to your left.

Continue on the Sunny Aspen Trail, which descends to the southwest. Although highway noise is still audible, the trail gives a great sense of solitude. At 1.16 miles, switchback to the northeast and descend more steeply on an old road. A trail sign directs you to the right at 1.24 miles. At 1.32 miles, go left on the Lodge Pole Trail, continuing your moderately steep descent. Switchback to the west at 1.36 miles and to the north at 1.45 miles. At 1.65 miles, continue straight, ignoring an old road that comes in from the right. You can now see U.S. 285 to the left through the trees. Pass a covered bench at 1.85 miles. The trail curves east across a small meadow. Keep to the left at 1.89 miles as another road comes in from the right. At 1.99 miles, turn left onto the Owl's Perch Trail, which descends along the west side of the picnic area. There is a bench at 2.12 miles. Turn left at the Owl's Perch Trail sign at 2.15 miles. Continue on down to the parking area.

Reynolds Park

This park is named for the Reynolds family, which gave much of its 1,260 acres to Jefferson County in 1975. The area was one of the first settled in Colorado, and the ranch house served as a stop both for pack trains traveling between Denver and Leadville and for the Pony Express. Between 1913 and 1942, the Idylease dude ranch operated here. Later, the property served as a cattle ranch.

The park, part of Jefferson County Open Space, has 5.9 miles of trails, some running through a valley and others high on surrounding steep slopes. Wildflowers, aspen, scrub oak, maple, and several species of conifer are found here. Wild turkey, black bear, grouse, deer, and elk are some of the resident wildlife. The hiking loop we describe combines some interesting high views with a forest trail. In places, the ascents are quite steep, so be well conditioned before you attempt them.

22. The Hummingbird and Songbird Trails

DEGREE OF DIFFICULTY: Moderate
ROUND-TRIP DISTANCE: 2.70 miles
ROUND-TRIP TIME: 1 hour 45 minutes
STARTING ALTITUDE: 7,200 feet
ELEVATION GAIN: Approximately 400 feet
MAP: Reynolds Park brochure

Getting There: From the junction of U.S. 285 and C-470, drive west on U.S. 285 South for 14.8 miles to a stoplight on the highway in Conifer. At 0.6 mile beyond, turn left on Foxton Road just past a sign for the Reynolds Open Space Park. Descend about 1,000 feet in 5.7 miles to the second large, unpaved parking area on the right. Picnic tables are adjacent, and a map box is available at the northwest end of the lot. The Hummingbird Trail begins just across the highway.

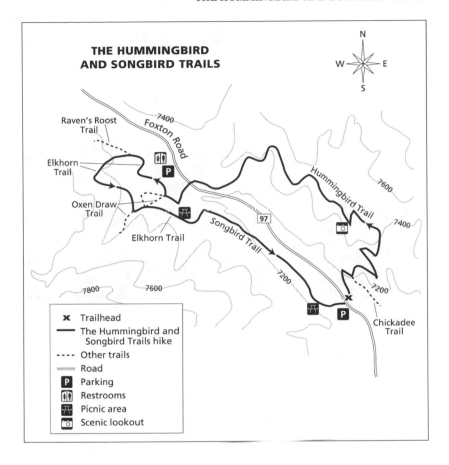

The Hike: The trail heads steeply uphill to the north-east. At 0.08 mile, the Chickadee Trail goes off to the right. Stay left and continue your steep ascent, which switches direction frequently. Pikes Peak comes into view, followed by the valley in the opposite direction. At 0.39 mile, the trail enters a conifer forest and the ascent becomes gentler. Pass through several switchbacks with good views to the south and west. The trail meanders under a power line, crossing it at 0.67, 0.75, and 0.78 mile. At 0.86 mile, head

Reynolds Park, with Pikes Peak in the distance.

downhill, looping to the north and then west. Go straight at a sign at 0.99 mile and descend with care on the steep trail. You will reach Foxton Road at 1.31 miles, opposite the first unpaved parking area.

Cross Foxton Road and go to the south end of the lot to a gate at 1.37 miles. Just beyond, there are picnic tables, a box of maps, a water pump, and a signboard with a map. The trail leads to some very clean toilets. You will reach the Elkhorn Trail at 1.40 miles. There may be maps in a box here with descriptions of the 21 interpretive nature stations along this trail. Go to the right through a wooded area and across a stream, and ascend past the Oxen Draw Trail on your left. There is a bench at 1.71 miles. Keep straight on the Elkhorn Trail past the Raven's Roost Trail on the right. Descend to the south gradually. At 1.93 miles, there is a junction with the Oxen Draw Trail again (the trails merge for a time), but continue straight on Elkhorn. At 1.98 miles, the Oxen Draw Trail goes left, but again, stay on Elkhorn. At 2.19 miles, past Station 5, there is a bench. The Songbird Trail heads south from here; descend on it to a bridge over a stream at 2.65 miles. The parking lot is only 0.05 mile beyond.

Elk Meadow Park

Now a 1,385-acre park, this area was homesteaded in 1869. A barn in the meadow dates from the early 1900s, a reminder that this was pastureland for herds of cattle. Joggers, bikers, horseback riders, cross-country skiers, and snowshoers as well as hikers use this easily accessible park, part of Jefferson County Open Space. In the fall, the Mt. Evans elk herd moves down here. Wildflowers are abundant in the spring. Hawks are frequently spotted, hunting small mammals that live in the meadow. Dwarf mistletoe is a common pine parasite. When its seeds germinate, the mistletoe fruiting bodies tap into the feeding system of the trees, stealing nutrients necessary for the tree's health and vigor. Heavily affected trees die and must be cut down to minimize further mistletoe spread.

The following hike loops around the perimeter of Elk Meadow. Our hiking times were about 30 minutes longer at various points along the way compared to those given in a popular trail guide. The trail length and the altitude have led us to label the degree of difficulty as moderate.

23. The Painter's Pause Trail/ Meadow View Trail Loop

DEGREE OF DIFFICULTY: Moderate
ROUND-TRIP DISTANCE: 4.18 miles
ROUND-TRIP TIME: 2 hours 15 minutes
STARTING ALTITUDE: 7,600 feet
ELEVATION GAIN: Approximately 510 feet
MAP: Elk Meadow Park brochure

Getting There: From the U.S. 285/C-470 junction, go west on C-470 for 6.3 miles to its termination at I-70. Continue west on I-70 for 9.4 miles to Exit 252 (Evergreen Parkway). Turn left, and go straight onto Colorado Highway 74. Travel east for 5.2 miles, just past a sign for Elk Meadow Open Space Park, and make a right turn on Lewis Ridge Road. After 0.2 mile, enter an unpaved parking area.

An alternate route is to take U.S. 285 South 1.9 miles past its junction with C-470 to the Evergreen–Morrison–Colorado Highway 8 exit. Turn right onto Colorado Highway 8 and continue for 2.3 miles, then turn left at a stoplight onto Colorado Highway 74 toward Evergreen. The road winds up Bear Creek Canyon through Idledale and Kittredge for 8.8 miles to the first stoplight in Evergreen. Proceed 3.1 miles farther on Highway 74 to Lewis Ridge Road and turn left. Go 0.2 mile to the unpaved parking lot.

The Hike: From the north end of the parking lot, walk 90 feet past some portable toilets to a signboard with an area map and a box of park brochures. Continue north, and just before you reach a covered bench, veer right at 0.05 mile. Arrive at the Painter's Pause Trail at 0.16 mile. The

trail you have been on is now identified as the Sleepy S Trail. Turn left on Painter's Pause, which parallels the noisy highway. There are lovely views to the left of the meadow and Bergen Peak (9,708 feet). Some parts of the trail are built up over wet areas. The trail ascends gently past a wooden barn and reaches a bench at 0.54 mile. Birdhouses are scattered throughout the meadow. The average grade here is said to be 4 percent.

Mt. Bergen, Elk Meadow Park.

At 1.17 miles, go left on the Meadow View Trail, ignoring the Bergen Park Trail to the right. The average grade on Meadow View is 3 percent. Move west away from the highway and toward the wooded slopes. At 1.39 miles, enter the conifers. You will reach a bench overlooking the meadow at 1.51 miles. Continue to climb the east base of Bergen Peak through some switchbacks, and at 2.06 miles note the Too Long Trail to the right. There is a bench at 2.07 miles. You will reach the high point of the hike (approximately 8,140 feet) at 2.11 miles.

Descending now, the path frequently heads down one side of a gully and up the other. The trail finally curves south, moves into some aspen, and crosses a small bridge at 2.55 miles. At 2.56 miles, there is a bench. You now walk in the forest on a needle-strewn path. At 3.08 miles, go left on the Elk Ridge Trail near another bench. The grade here is said to be 14 percent, much of it rocky. Descend through several switchbacks, and at 3.61 miles go left on the Sleepy S Trail near a bench. Arrive back at the covered bench at 4.11 miles and veer to the right toward the parking lot.

Roxborough State Park

Despite its proximity to Denver, this 3,299-acre scenic transition area between the plains and the mountains remains seemingly undiscovered by metro Denver residents. Established as a state park in 1986, it is also a designated Colorado Natural Area and a National Natural Landmark. The efforts of many environmentalists, particularly the Roxborough Park Foundation, have protected the park from encroachment by adjacent housing developments.

The park's most striking feature is its tilted slabs of 310-million-year-old red sandstone from the Fountain Formation, exposed by gradual erosion of the original Rocky Mountains. Two more sedimen- tary rock ridges, the Lyons Formation and the Dakota Hogback, 250 and 135 million years old respectively, lie to the east. About 65–70 million years ago, a major geological uplift took place here over sev- eral million years. Erosion by wind and water sculpted the fantastic rock shapes seen today. The granite atop nearby Carpenter Peak has been dated variously as 0.5–1.5 billion years old.

Signs of early hunters (12,000–9,500 BCE) have been found just east of the park. There is evidence that Plains Apache, Comanche, Ute, Cheyenne, and Arapaho hunted and fought in this area. A member of Major Stephen Long's expedition was the first person we know of to record sighting Roxborough in 1820. William Henry Jackson photographed the sandstone slabs in 1873, two years after the first homestead claim was filed. In 1902, Henry Persse, a businessman and real estate developer, assembled the properties that had been known as Washington Park and renamed the area Roxborough after his family estate in Ireland. He planned to develop homesites and a resort, but the latter never came to fruition. For a brief period in the early 1900s, brick-making flourished here, as did the production of illegal whiskey during Prohibition.

The park's plants, birds, and wildlife are remarkably varied and prolific. Yucca and cactus grow near aspen, wild roses, and Mariposa lilies. Medicinal plants, such as licorice, and poisonous ones, such as hemlock and poison ivy, flourish here. Approximately 40 different bird species, including golden and bald eagles, osprey, and wild turkey, make their home in the park, as do occasional rattlesnakes, bear, and mountain lions, along with the more common mule deer, elk, black and red fox, prairie dogs, bobcats, weasels, voles, and coyotes. Several butterfly species live here, including the state butterfly, the Colorado Hairstreak.

Descriptions of three progressively more difficult hikes follow. The 1.5-mile Willow Creek Trail has been omitted because it is extremely hot much of the year and is less interesting than the other trails. Water and restrooms are available only at the visitors center, which features a number of interesting exhibits, a good selection of books, and brochures about naturalist-guided activities such as bird walks and hikes. Hikes focus on a particular theme, among them geology, history, archaeology, wildflowers, wildlife, and nature. The patio has a lovely rock garden and several informative signs.

24. Fountain Valley Trail

DEGREE OF DIFFICULTY: Easy
ROUND-TRIP DISTANCE: 2.12 miles, skipping both overlooks;
    2.37 miles, including both overlooks
ROUND-TRIP TIME: 60 minutes, skipping both overlooks
STARTING ALTITUDE: 6,200 feet (visitors center)
ELEVATION GAIN: 200 feet (at Lyons Overlook)
MAP: Roxborough State Park brochure

The Fountain Valley Loop Trail Guide, obtained at the visitors center for $1, is an excellent companion at the 20 educational stops along this short but highly interesting hike. Though it takes only about an hour to hike the dirt-and-gravel road (wide enough for a passenger-cart train carrying disabled persons), much more time is needed to fully absorb all the information provided in the guide.

Getting There: You have two options.

1. Take C-470 to Wadsworth Boulevard (Colorado Highway 121). Go south on Wadsworth for 4.6 miles and make a left turn on Waterton Road. Proceed 1.7 miles to the Rampart Range Road. Turn right and go 2.3 miles before making a left turn onto the gravel Roxborough Park Road. At 0.1 mile down this road, turn right, past a fire station, and drive 0.5 mile to the park entrance station. A daily or annual state parks pass can be purchased here or, if the station is closed, at a self-service box 0.5 mile into the park. From the entrance station, travel 1.2 miles to a paved road

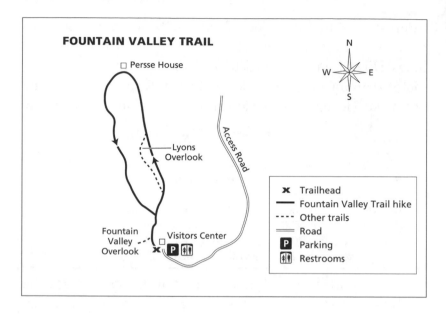

at the park entrance. Parking lots are 0.6 and 0.8 mile beyond. From these, a somewhat steep 0.1-mile paved walk
leads to the visitors center.

2. Drive south on Santa Fe Drive (U.S. 85) 4.4 miles beyond its junction with C-470 to a stoplight at Titan Road
(Douglas County Road #7). Turn right and drive 3.2 miles
to where the road curves left and becomes the Rampart
Range Road (Douglas County Road #5). After 1.3 more
miles, you will come to a stop sign at the intersection of
Waterton and Rampart Range Roads. Continue straight on
Rampart Range Road for 2.3 more miles and make a left
turn onto the gravel Roxborough Park Road. From this
point, follow the directions in Option 1.

The Hike: The trail starts just north of the visitors center. An aerial map of much of Roxborough Park is displayed
100 feet down on the left. The trail ascends gradually. At

0.12 mile, there is a 150-foot path on the left to the Fountain Valley Overlook, where benches are located. From here, there is a fine view to the north, encompassing the sandstone slabs, Carpenter Peak, and the entire Fountain Formation. At approximately 0.20 mile, the road splits. We recommend taking the right fork, because the ascent on the return trip will be easier. The trail can get very hot on a midsummer afternoon. At approximately 0.50 mile, a moderately steep 0.15-mile trail on the left ascends to the Lyons Overlook (bench available), where again the views are lovely. This is the highest point on the hike. Return to the main trail and continue north.

At 0.60 mile, there is a bench under a tree. A gentle descent leads to the reconstructed Persse House, originally built at the turn of the twentieth century. Nearby are some collapsed wooden ranch buildings. The trail now swings to the southwest past a sign reminding hikers that this is rattlesnake country. It then crosses a stream and climbs gradually. Another bench is located at 1.64 miles. From this point back to the fork in the road, you walk among striking rock formations. Bear, deer, and elk tracks are seen frequently on the trail. Continue south to the starting point.

25. The South Rim Trail

DEGREE OF DIFFICULTY: Easy from the north end; moderate from the south end
ROUND-TRIP DISTANCE: 3.00 miles
ROUND-TRIP TIME: 1 hour 30 minutes
STARTING ALTITUDE: 6,100 feet from the south end; 6,200 feet from the north end
ELEVATION GAIN: 475 feet from the south end; 375 feet from the north end
MAP: Roxborough State Park brochure

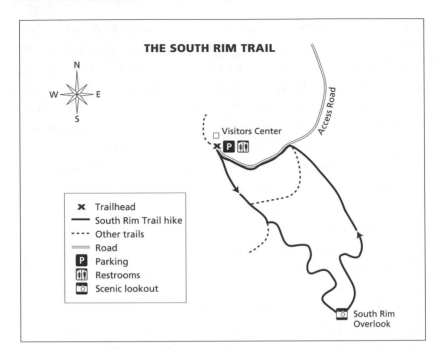

This is one of our favorite hikes close to Denver because the views are magnificent and the trail, popular with runners, can be hiked from early spring until significant snow falls. It is easier to start from the north end of the trail, just opposite the visitors center, than from the south end below the lower parking lot, as the ascent is more gradual. We will describe the hike in both directions.

Getting There: The directions are the same as for the Fountain Valley Trail (Hike #24).

The Hike: You may begin at either end of the trail.

Starting from the north end of the trail: Begin just west of the visitors center at the sign for the Willow Creek Loop, South Rim Loop, and Carpenter Peak Trail. The trail initially cuts through scrub oak. Almost immediately, a sign on the left explains how to recognize poison ivy, which grows in the park. A bench is located at 0.07 mile. The trail gently ascends and descends. At intervals, numbered signposts for the Willow Creek Loop correlate with information found in an inexpensive booklet available at the visitors center.

The trail bends southeast, and at 0.15 mile you begin moving in and out of the scrub oak. Pass a bench at 0.17 mile. Soon excellent views of the South Rim (to the southeast) and the red rock slabs (to the southwest) open up. At nearly 0.50 mile, the Willow Creek Trail goes off to the left; continue straight ahead on the South Rim and Carpenter Peak Trails. Emerge from the scrub and proceed to a fork at 0.54 mile. The South Rim path goes to the left; the one to Carpenter Peak and the Colorado Trail veers right.

At 0.57 mile, a bench sits under a cottonwood tree. The trail now turns slightly eastward and descends to a small wooden bridge over a stream at 0.63 mile. Ascend gradually to a bench at 0.75 mile. Re-enter the scrub at 0.76 mile. The trail now ascends a bit more steeply in short traverses. At 1.03 miles, there is a wonderful view of the red rock slabs to the north and west. Additional benches are located at 1.04 and 1.10 miles. Evergreens now begin to appear among the scrub bushes. The trail becomes steeper as you climb through switchbacks to the top of the South Rim. At 1.40 miles, head northeast and savor a good view of the park. Several huge, multistoried homes have been built west of the park. At 1.50 miles, the trail breaks out onto a ledge, offering an even more spectacular view of the park and foothills. At 1.54 miles, the highest point on the trail, a

Red rock slabs from the South Rim Trail, Roxborough State Park.

short path leads to a bench and an unobstructed view to the east and north.

The trail now descends gradually to the northern crest of the South Rim, which has a beautiful panoramic view. The Aurora Rampart Reservoir and Dakota Ridge are straight ahead. At 1.65 miles, arrive at a small fence protecting a revegetation area. The trail now turns south and then east, descending somewhat more steeply. The impressive views continue.

The trail winds down the side of the South Rim, switchbacking at 2.01 and 2.12 miles. Mule deer are often seen on adjacent slopes. At 2.25 miles, there is another bench, and at 2.41 miles the Willow Creek Trail rejoins the one you are on. There is a bench at the junction.

Near its end, the trail re-enters scrub and curves east. At 2.57 miles, there is a bench just before a wooden bridge over a creek. The trail now ascends toward a small parking lot, crosses a gully, and ends at the road at 2.70 miles, next to a sign for the Willow Creek and South Rim Trails. Cross the road and continue on a trail to the parking lots. A bench is located at 2.71 miles. The lower parking lot, with restrooms, is 0.10 mile farther. You will reach the upper parking lot, with a bench, at 2.90 miles.

Starting from the south end of the trail: Approximately 500 feet south of the lower parking lot, look for a sign on the west side of the road, indicating the Willow Creek and South Rim Trails. Follow this path. At 450 feet, cross a wooden bridge over a small stream. The trail ascends through stands of scrub oak. At 0.35 mile, the trail splits. Take the left fork heading up to the South Rim (ignore the right-fork path to Willow Creek). Many wildflowers, including Mariposa lilies, can be seen in the spring adjacent to the trail. Benches are located at 0.40, 1.10, 1.55, 1.90, 2.10, 2.50, and 2.60 miles. At 0.40 mile, the red rock slabs of the Fountain Formation to the west become visible. As you ascend and the trail switchbacks, the views of the slabs and the Front Range become more impressive.

At 1.02 miles, there is an overlook near the top of the rim, with terrific views of the plains to the east, and the park and Front Range to the north and west. At 1.12 miles, arrive at the top of the trail. A short path off to the east again offers fine vistas of Denver and the plains. The trail now descends, sometimes in gentle switchbacks, entering Fountain Valley at 1.90 miles. At 2.12 miles, the trail joins

the main path back to the visitors center. Reach your starting point in the lower parking lot at 3.00 miles.

26. Carpenter Peak

> DEGREE OF DIFFICULTY: Moderate
> ROUND-TRIP DISTANCE: 6.44 miles
> ROUND-TRIP TIME: 4 hours 10 minutes (2 hours 25 minutes
>   up, 1 hour 45 minutes down)
> STARTING ALTITUDE: 6,200 feet (visitors center)
> ELEVATION GAIN: 920 feet
> Maps: Roxborough State Park brochure, USGS Kassler
>   Quadrangle Map

This 7,205-foot peak is named for an early settler. The
first half mile of the hike duplicates the beginning of the
South Rim hike, starting at the north end of that loop. You
should carry lots of water, as the trail can be quite hot in
summer, even as early as 9:00 A.M. Be aware that the trail
is rather steep in places, so older hikers who are unacclimated or have knee or hip problems should go slowly and
cautiously at times. The rewards for climbing up high are
the wonderful views, not only of the park and plains but
also the many snow-covered peaks to the west.

Getting There: The directions are the same as for the
Fountain Valley Trail (Hike #24).

The Hike: The trail begins just west of the visitors center at a sign for the Willow Creek Loop, the South Rim
Loop, and the Carpenter Peak Trail. The dirt path initially
cuts through scrub oak. Almost immediately a sign on the
left explains how to recognize poison ivy, which is found in
the park. A bench is located at 0.07 mile. The trail gently
ascends and descends. At intervals, numbered signposts
for the Willow Creek Loop correlate with information found

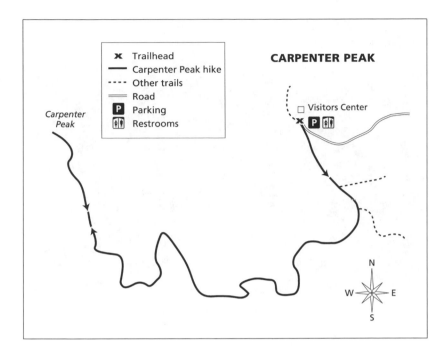

in an inexpensive booklet available at the visitors center.

The trail bends southeast, and at 0.15 mile you begin moving in and out of scrub oak. Pass a bench at 0.17 mile. Soon excellent views of the South Rim (to the southeast) and the red rock slabs (to the southwest) open up. At nearly 0.50 mile, the Willow Creek Trail goes off to the left; continue straight on the South Rim and Carpenter Peak Trails. You emerge from the scrub, and at 0.54 mile the trail forks. The South Rim path goes to the left; take the right hand fork to Carpenter Peak and the Colorado Trail.

The ascent now becomes more pronounced. A sign at 0.60 mile announces that you are 2.6 miles from Carpenter Peak. At 0.62 mile, a notice warns of mountain lion activity in this area and instructs you to face the lion, back away

Roxborough State Park from the Carpenter Peak Trail.

slowly, look large, raise your arms, and, if necessary, fight back. As you continue to climb, you can see the south end of Fountain Valley, with an abandoned cabin. The ascent becomes even steeper as you climb to the northwest and then, at 0.80 mile, turn south again. The trail switchbacks three times between 1.04 and 1.16 miles. As you move higher on the east face of the ridge, you will come upon good views of the park and the Denver skyline. At 1.20 miles, enter an area of scrub oak. The trail continues to climb around gullies and ridges. At 1.30 miles, you travel due west among evergreens. A bit beyond this, there is a bench.

The switchbacks continue, and at 1.33 miles you gain an even more impressive view of the park. This section of the trail is quite steep in places. At 1.53 miles, views to the north and east are once again excellent. You encounter more switchbacks, and finally, at about 1.60 miles your goal, the top of Carpenter Peak, appears. You now walk among evergreens. The trail curves west around a gully at 1.87 miles, then ascends over a ridge. A bench is located a few feet beyond this point, at 2.06 miles.

There is now a moderately steep descent for about 400 feet. Continue downhill more gradually until the trail again turns upward at 2.25 miles. Encounter a steep section at 2.51 miles. Five hundred feet beyond this, there are rock steps leading down a gully and up the other side. At 2.92 miles, there is another bench with excellent views east and down into the park. At 3.12 miles, the trail forks. Ignore the left fork, which leads to the Colorado Trail (4.40 miles), Waterton Canyon (3.00 miles), and the Waterton Canyon parking area. Instead, take the right fork, which heads up a steep and rocky trail 0.10 mile to Carpenter Peak. Climb the rocks at the end of the trail to the top. There are flat places and rocks to sit on and enjoy the 360-degree panoramic view—you've certainly earned it.

Castlewood Canyon State Park

It's hard to believe that Cherry Creek, usually a shallow, slow-flowing stream, could have cut Castlewood Canyon down through the Arkansas Divide, a 40-by-75-mile high grassland that includes the Black Forest north of Colorado Springs. However, millions of years of erosion have produced this canyon, which is several hundred feet deep in places.

The canyon walls are formed of sandstone, limestone, and conglomerate comprising hardened layers of sediment and rocks brought here by shallow seas, flooding rivers, and volcanic eruptions eons ago. Cherry Creek originates about 10 miles south of the park, near the 7,400-foot Palmer Divide, and flows north through the Black Forest and the canyon it cut to Denver, where it joins the South Platte River at Confluence Park.

The park is home to five ecosystems—grassland, caprock, shrubland, conifer-forest, and riparian—and a diverse flora and fauna.

The remains of Castlewood Dam constitute the park's most noteworthy historical feature. The dam was built by a private company in 1890 to store 200 surface acres of water intended for irrigation use over thousands of acres of adjacent land. Safety questions arose almost immediately, and in 1891 the state engineer found that the rock rubble dam, 83 feet thick at its base, 65 feet tall, and 630 feet long, had been built on inadequate footings. In 1897 and again in 1899, sections of the top of the dam washed out. Despite repairs, more leaks continued to appear. On the morning of August 3, 1933, after several days of rain filled the reservoir, the dam broke, releasing a 15-foot wall of water that carried tons of debris, livestock, and boulders down the canyon. Fortunately, notification was sent promptly to Denver, saving many lives. Lower sections of the city flooded, bridges and buildings were swept away, and Market Street was under 3 feet of water. This was Denver's second-worst flood, causing two deaths and over $1 million in damage.

In 1980, this state park opened for day use. A visitors center with restrooms, drinking water, books for sale, and several excellent murals and displays was added in 1993. Naturalist tours originate here throughout the year.

Two of the three hikes we describe here have been modified for seniors. We feel that the Inner Canyon Trail and the Rim Rock Trail are too rocky for older hikers to negotiate safely. Although two of the hikes end at the same place near the remains of the dam, they approach it from different directions. These hikes are best done in spring, as the canyon is too hot for comfort in summer. In addition, water flow is minimal during summer and autumn months.

27. Bridge Canyon Overlook and Canyon View Nature Trail

DEGREE OF DIFFICULTY: Easy
ROUND-TRIP DISTANCE: 0.20 mile (Bridge Canyon Overlook); 1.00 mile (Canyon View Nature Trail)
ROUND-TRIP TIME: 15 minutes (Bridge Canyon Overlook); 45 minutes (Canyon View Nature Trail)
STARTING ALTITUDE: 6,400 feet (visitors center)
ELEVATION GAIN: Approximately 100 feet after descent
MAP: Castlewood Canyon State Park brochure

Getting There: From its junction with C-470, go south on I-25 for 12.5 miles to Exit 182. The turnoff is preceded by a sign for Wilcox Street and Wolfensberger Road, followed by another for Franktown and Colorado Highway 86. At the top of the exit ramp, turn left and go 0.1 mile to a stoplight, then turn right onto Highway 86 (Wilcox Street). Drive 1.0 mile, and at Fifth Street turn left onto Highway 86 going east toward Franktown. After 6.5 miles, turn right onto Colorado Highway 83 southbound. At 4.0 miles down this road, note the magnificent view of Pikes

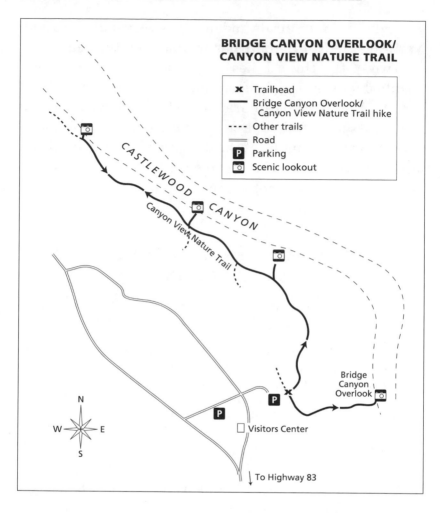

Peak. At 5.0 miles, make a right turn into the park (25.1 miles from the C-470/I-25 junction). The entrance station is 0.7 mile farther. A left turn takes you to the visitors center; a right turn takes you into the parking lot for the Bridge Canyon Overlook and Canyon View Nature Trail.

The Hike: The combination of both trails results in a pleasant and informative 1.20-mile walk. The Bridge Canyon Overlook is marked by a sign at the south end of the parking lot. A 0.10-mile paved walk leads down to a gazebo from which steps descend to a wooden observation platform. There are excellent views of the canyon to the north, Cherry Creek, and a bridge to the south. The bridge was built in 1946 and is said to span more than 40 million years of geologic history. Retrace your steps to the parking lot.

A few feet north, near some water fountains, there is a sign for the Canyon View Nature Trail. The Juniper Rock picnic area is just north of the parking lot. The nature trail is paved and descends gently to three photo and viewing areas. You will reach the first at 0.15 mile and the second at 0.30 mile. Just beyond the third, at 0.50 mile, is a bench. Educational signs and good views make this a worthwhile walk. Retrace your steps to the parking lot and spend some time at the visitors center, learning more about the park.

28. Lake Gulch Trail to the Castlewood Dam Ruins

DEGREE OF DIFFICULTY: Easy
ROUND-TRIP DISTANCE: 2.40 miles
ROUND-TRIP TIME: 1 hour 15 minutes
STARTING ALTITUDE: 6,600 feet
ELEVATION GAIN: Approximately 100 feet after descent
MAP: Castlewood Canyon State Park brochure

Getting There: Follow the directions for the Bridge Canyon Overlook and Canyon View Nature Trail (Hike #27) up to the entrance station. However, instead of turning right into the parking lot, continue straight toward Canyon Point, 0.5 mile farther on. Park in the large lot, which

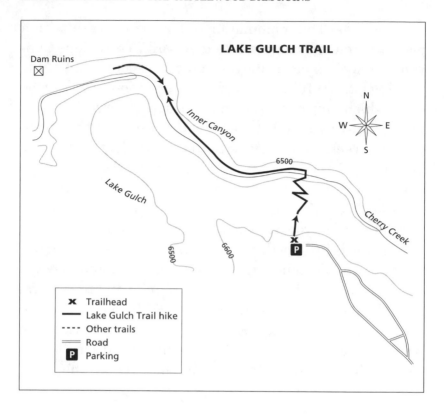

has toilets, drinking water, and a large group picnic area just to the north.

The Hike: The Lake Gulch Trail begins adjacent to this picnic area and gradually descends to the north and east. At 0.20 mile, pass a trail to the left that leads to the Pikes Peak Amphitheater. Descend farther on several switchbacks that have wonderful views of Pikes Peak. At 0.40 mile, a short path to the left leads to a view of a pretty valley to the northwest. The descent now becomes a bit steeper and rockier as it heads down to Cherry Creek, which you cross at about 0.80 mile on a wooden bridge. Ascend a few steps and turn left. Ignore a sign indicating the Inner Canyon Trail to the right. Just beyond you on the trail is a sign stating that the dam ruins are 0.3 mile ahead. At 1.10 miles, you can see them. Ascend several steps to a view point at 1.20 miles, from which you can look down on the ruins, Cherry Creek, and the Creek Bottom Trail coming in from the north. Retrace your steps to the parking lot.

29. Creek Bottom Trail to the Castlewood Dam Ruins

DEGREE OF DIFFICULTY: Easy
ROUND-TRIP DISTANCE: 2.56 miles
ROUND-TRIP TIME: 1 hour 20 minutes
STARTING ALTITUDE: 6,300 feet
ELEVATION GAIN: 100 feet
MAP: Castlewood Canyon State Park brochure

Getting There: Use the same directions as for Hike #27 up through the left turn from Wilcox Street onto Colorado Highway 86 (Fifth Street). Drive east on Highway 86 toward Franktown for 6.1 miles and make a right turn (south) onto Castlewood Canyon Road. The pavement gives way to a dirt road at 0.6 mile. After an additional 1.6 miles, enter the park. Drive for 1.0 mile, passing the Homestead parking area, to the West Side Trailhead parking area. Toilets and picnic tables are available here.

The Hike: The dirt Creek Bottom Trail begins just to the right (south) of the toilets. A signboard and several picnic tables and benches are just beyond. The trail heads off to the right and gradually winds farther south near the road to the Falls Trailhead parking area at 0.18 mile. Gradually descend toward Cherry Creek. At approximately 0.30 mile, a sign indicates that the Creek Bottom Trail runs

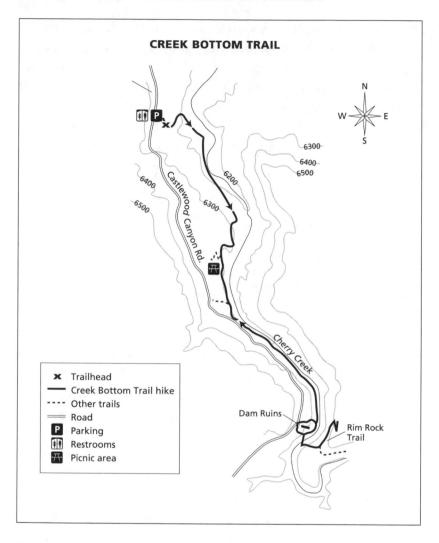

both left and right. Head to the right. Almost immediately, you can see and hear the 30- to 40-foot waterfall. The path takes you down a series of wooden steps at 0.34 mile. Continue south as the trail angles back and forth. It is likely

Dam remains, Castlewood Canyon State Park.

that you will see many hawks wheeling overhead. Several forks veer off to the left, but keep right on the trail.

At 0.57 mile, you are at creek level, with high canyon walls to the left and conifers to the right. Continue upstream. At 0.85 mile, you can see the dam ruins. The trail passes under an eroded rocky slope with many projecting boulders, so it is a good idea to move through here quickly.

At just about 1.00 mile, rock steps take you to a sign (which you ignore) indicating the steep Dam Historic Trail up to the right. Continue down several wooden steps and go right under the dam ruins. At 1.10 miles, pick up the south end of the Dam Historic Trail on your right. Just beyond, cross Cherry Creek on a 50-foot wooden bridge that bounces alarmingly as you walk and cautiously ascend many wooden steps through an eroded area to a sign at 1.20 miles. The sign indicates the Inner Canyon Trail to the right, which you should ignore, and the Rim Rock Trail, which you want, to the left. Ascend more wooden steps and take a short trail to the left that passes huge stone blocks on the east side of the dam ruins at 1.28 miles. You can now look down on the ruins and the creek as well as southwest into a lovely valley. Retrace your steps to the parking lot.

Golden Gate Canyon State Park

Beginning in 1960, parcels of land were purchased to establish Golden Gate Canyon State Park, which now comprises more than 14,000 acres and approximately 35 miles of hiking trails. The area was frequented some 12,000–7,500 years ago by hunters of mammoth and bison, and subsequently by hunters of deer, elk, rabbit, and bison, as well as gatherers of roots, berries, and seeds. About 400–500 years ago, Ute from the mountains, and Cheyenne, Arapaho, Comanche, Apache, and Kiowa from the plains visited this area. Fur trappers came to the region for beaver in the early 1800s. The discovery of gold in May 1859 near Black Hawk and Central City, six miles south of the park, brought miners and settlers pouring into this area. The Golden Gate Canyon Toll Road was opened within a month as a gateway to the goldfields. Wagons cost $.50 one way, but no toll was charged if the occupants were going to church or a funeral. The 15-mile road was so steep that a team of 20 oxen was needed to pull a half-ton wagon

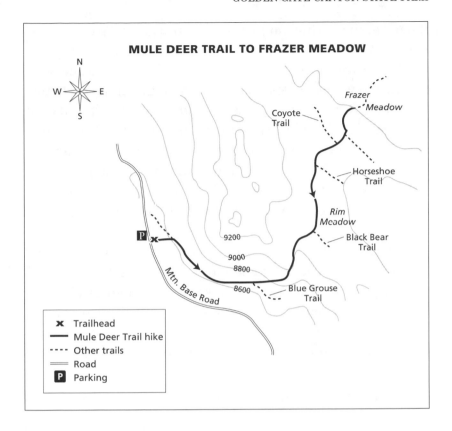

up, and huge trees were attached to slow the wagons on their descent.

By 1861, a more direct road was built through Clear Creek Canyon, and the toll road deteriorated. Logging, ranching, farming, and quartz mining continued to attract settlers prepared to stay. So intensive was the logging that almost all trees in the park today are second growth, with few more than 100 years old. Not well-known is the fact that during Prohibition, this area was the moonshine and bootlegging base for Denver and surrounding communities. It was said that so many local people were involved in this illegal activity that no jury in Gilpin County would hand down a conviction.

There are 12 major trails in the park, each named after an animal whose footprints mark the trail signs. Although the Park Service designates the degree of difficulty for these trails as moderate to most difficult, we respectfully disagree. What they call moderate, we would call hard for most seniors. What they call difficult, we would term next to impossible. The problem is both steepness of the trails and altitude, which varies from 7,400 feet to 10,388 feet. An additional detraction is that many of the trails have no interesting views, which in our opinion eliminates them. Having hiked several of the more promising trails, we offer one as a difficult hike with some worthwhile views. If you do go to the park, by all means carefully drive up Mountain Base Road (with a 19 percent grade in places) to Panorama Point, where one of the most spectacular mountain views in Colorado awaits you.

30. Mule Deer Trail to Frazer Meadow

DEGREE OF DIFFICULTY: Hard
ROUND-TRIP DISTANCE: 3.06 miles
ROUND-TRIP TIME: 2 hours 15 minutes
STARTING ALTITUDE: Approximately 8,500 feet
ELEVATION GAIN: Approximately 700 feet
MAP: Golden Gate Canyon State Park brochure

Getting There: From the junction of Wadsworth Boulevard (Colorado Highway 121) and 6th Avenue, go west on 6th Avenue (which becomes U.S. 6) 9.7 miles to where it runs straight into Colorado Highway 93. Proceed 3.5 more miles and make a left turn onto Golden Gate Canyon Road. After 10.0 miles on this narrow, winding road, a sign indi-

Mt. Tremont, Golden Gate Canyon State Park.

cates the park entrance. Head into the park and after 0.5 more mile, reach a visitors center with excellent displays. Go 1.5 miles farther on and turn right onto Mountain Base Road. Travel 0.9 mile to a sign on the right displaying the symbol of two deer hooves on a yellow background, just below the word "Trail." Opposite is a wide pullout for parking.

The Hike: Cross the road and start up the Mule Deer Trail. At 65 feet, there is a signboard with a map. The narrow dirt trail ascends steeply to the northeast, with pretty views down into the valley on your right. At 0.17 mile, enter a conifer-and-aspen forest. At 0.21 mile, pass the first of many metal posts that mark the trail. At 0.26 mile, another branch of the Mule Deer Trail comes in from the left. The ascent becomes increasingly steep and rocky. At 0.45

mile, the Blue Grouse Trail splits off to the right, but you continue to the left. At 0.53 mile, there are good views to the southwest. At 0.74 mile, enter an area of aspen. The Black Bear Trail goes off to the right at 0.94 mile, but you continue left to Frazer Meadow.

At 1.08 miles, Tremont Mountain (10,388 feet) looms ahead across the valley. The Horseshoe Trail runs off to the right at 1.20 miles, where a sign indicates that the trailhead is 1.1 miles behind you. Cross a small bridge over a stream at 1.30 miles and immediately come to a broken-down cabin. The ascent is now more gradual. At 1.40 miles, the Coyote Trail comes in from the left. At 1.53 miles, there is a clump of trees—a good stopping point for food and rest. Descend the way you came, but with care, as you now will be more impressed with the steepness of the trail.

Indian Peaks Wilderness

You may wonder why we have included a hike that takes less time to complete than the 1.5-hour drive to the trailhead from the Denver metro area. The reason is that it offers both spectacular and easily accessible mountain scenery and a high-altitude experience.

The hike to Mitchell Lake and beyond is in the Roosevelt National Forest near the town of Ward, settled in 1860 and named for the man who discovered the first profitable mine in the region. The area is managed by the National Forest Service, not run by the National Park Service. An entrance fee is required, which in the year 2000 was $5.00 per car or $2.50 for seniors with a Golden Age Passport. The name "Indian Peaks" refers to a group of more than 10 mountains that constitute the Continental Divide in this area. The peaks are named for Native American tribes such as the Arapaho, Pawnee, and Shoshoni. Many beautiful lakes are located here. Several hiking trails depart from the Brainard Lake (10,345 feet) Recreation Area, which has several picnic locations, toilet facilities, and an informative sign describing the area and the surrounding mountain panorama. In 1965, approximately 55,000 acres around the recreation area were closed to development and vehicles, and in 1978 the Indian Peaks Wilderness was established.

The spectacular scenery results from glacial carving and deposition of boulders and rock debris, which ended only about 15,000 years ago. Winter winds coming off the Continental Divide so chill the terrain that trees and plants on the east side of Brainard Lake have the stunted and twisted appearance of vegetation found 1,200 feet higher at timberline.

31. Mitchell Lake

DEGREE OF DIFFICULTY: Easy
ROUND-TRIP DISTANCE: 2.18 miles
ROUND-TRIP TIME: 1 hour 25 minutes (45 minutes up, 40 minutes down)
STARTING ALTITUDE: 10,345 feet (at Brainard Lake)
ELEVATION GAIN: 335 feet
MAPS: USGS Ward, Brainard Lake Recreation Area map

Getting There: Drive west to Nederland on Colorado Highway 119 (Canyon Road) 17.4 miles from its intersection with U.S. 36 (28th Street) in Boulder. At the traffic

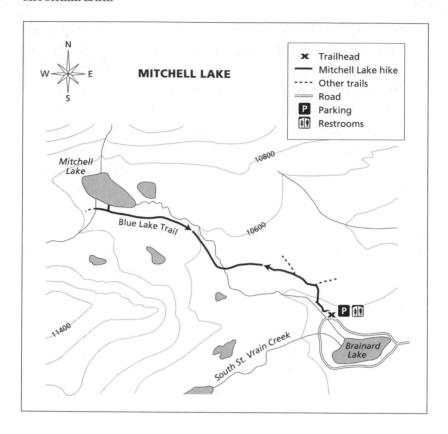

circle, turn right onto Colorado Highway 72 going west toward Estes Park. You will reach Ward at 11.9 miles. After
0.8 more mile, turn left at a sign on the right for the
Brainard Lake Recreation Area. The entrance station is
approximately 2.0 miles up the road. Almost immediately
beyond it is Red Rock Lake, a good place for a picnic. Continue on for approximately 3.0 more miles to a sign for the
Mitchell Lake parking area to the right. This lot, which
has toilet facilities, fills up very early during summer. The

Mitchell Lake, Indian Peaks Wilderness.

Mitchell and Blue Lake Trailhead is behind a signboard at the southwest corner of the lot.

The Hike: The signboard indicating the Mitchell Lake Trail #912 claims that Mitchell Lake is 1.0 mile away, Blue Lake 3.0 miles. Start on the dirt trail through the conifers. The ascent is gentle, but exercise care because the trail is rocky and full of large roots in places. There are blue markers high on trees to help skiers and snowshoers, but these end at the wilderness boundary. A great deal of deadfall lies adjacent to the trail.

At 0.30 mile, cross some planks over a small stream. In wet areas just beyond, you will encounter two more sets of planks. Cross a bridge over a creek at 0.43 mile and immediately reach two signs. One announces the Indian Peaks Wilderness, Arapaho/Roosevelt National Forest; the other states the wilderness regulations. At 0.49 mile, another plank bridge traverses a wet area. The trail is now steeper, the trees denser. At 0.84 mile, there is a trail marker; Mitchell Lake can now be seen to the northwest. Another trail marker is situated at 0.86 mile. A short trail to the right at 0.88 mile leads down to the lake. Towering above it are Mt. Toll (12,929 feet), Paiute Peak (13,088 feet), and Audubon Peak (13,223 feet).

If you wish to hike a bit more, regain the trail that leads into the trees along the south side of the lake. At 0.99 mile, another trail to the right goes down to the lake. On the main trail at 1.09 miles, arrive at a rapidly flowing creek spanned by two logs. From here, the trail continues for about 1.5 miles to Blue Lake, but we usually stop here and retrace our steps to the parking lot.

Chief Mountain

32. Chief Mountain

DEGREE OF DIFFICULTY: Hard
ROUND-TRIP DISTANCE: 3.44 miles
ROUND-TRIP TIME: 2 hours 30 minutes (1 hour 30 minutes up, 1 hour down)
STARTING ALTITUDE: Approximately 10,700 feet
ELEVATION GAIN: Approximately 1,000 feet
MAPS: USGS Idaho Springs, Clear Creek County

The major attractions of this hike are the wonderful panoramic views from the summit and the

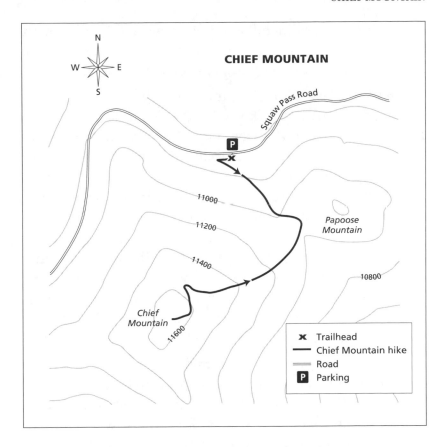

sense of achievement derived from making it to a moun-
taintop. While the climb might be difficult for some seniors,
it is far easier than many peaks we have attempted. From
the top, you can see Pikes Peak to the southeast; Mt. Evans
to the southwest; Gray's and Torrey's Peaks to the west;
James, South Arapaho, and Longs Peaks to the northwest;
and the plains to the east.

Most guidebooks suggest a starting point that requires
a very steep 0.2-mile scramble up to the trailhead. We have
tried this several times and don't like it. Our modification

gets you to the trailhead on an old road in 0.5 mile—a bit longer but a more gradual and less strenuous ascent. We list the hike as hard only because of the altitude.

Getting There: From its junction with U.S. 285, take C-470 west 6.3 miles to I-70 west. After 9.3 miles, turn off at Exit 252 (Evergreen Parkway) and go 0.7 mile to a stoplight. Continue straight onto Colorado Highway 74 east for 2.9 miles and turn right onto Squaw Pass Road (Colorado Highway 103). This is also called the Mt. Evans Road. Squaw Mountain, with antennas on its top, is straight ahead. At 11.3 miles, Chief Mountain is visible from the road. At 12.5 miles, turn left onto the upper of two dirt roads heading east. This rocky, unpaved road goes to the top of Squaw Mountain, but a passenger car can easily be driven up it for 0.4 mile to a wide area where it is joined by another dirt road coming up from the left. Park by metal post 192.1.

The Hike: Just opposite the metal post, you will see the unpaved Old Squaw Pass Road sloping up to the west. The first few feet have eroded, but it is an easy, short scramble to access the road. The ascent is gradual, with conifers growing alongside the road and sometimes in it. The snow-capped Continental Divide is visible to the right. At 0.50 mile, look for a wooden sign up and to the left that marks the trailhead. The sign can be difficult to see if there are shadows on it. It indicates that Chief Mountain is 2.0 miles ahead, but actually it is only 1.22 miles. Head east up the moderately steep, rocky trail through the pines. At 0.68 and 0.69 mile, two cairns mark the left side of the trail as you proceed up the saddle between Chief Mountain on the west and Papoose Mountain on the east.

At 0.85 mile, the trail switchbacks to the north-west and ascends across the north face of Chief Mountain. At 1.22 miles, leave the trees for the lower tundra, with its stunted pines. Just beyond, if you look up to the left, you will see the rocky knob of the summit. At 1.24 miles, begin several switchbacks that take you up to the top. Squaw Mountain is behind you. There is a lot of loose rock on the trail near the top, so be careful. At 1.71 miles, reach a saddle and look right at Mt. Evans across a valley. A very short scramble over some rocks to the right (north) puts you at the summit (11,709 feet), where there are places to sit and enjoy the magnificent views. Descend the way you came.

Rocky Mountain National Park

A National Park Service brochure states that "Rocky Mountain is a park for hikers," and so it is. It contains more than 355 miles of trails of all degrees of difficulty, including six self-guided interpretive trails (brochures available at the trailhead or the visitors centers). The park covers 414 square miles; contains 20 mountains over 13,000 feet, including 14,255-foot Longs Peak; encompasses more than 150 lakes; and is bisected by the highest continuous paved highway in the United States, Trail Ridge Road. Alpine glaciers, which flowed until approximately 10,000 years ago, cut valleys, gorges, and lake depressions in the mountains, which rose to their present height millions of years ago. Deer, elk, big-horn sheep, marmot, coyote, beaver, pika, and occasional moose, bear, and mountain lions live here, as do innumerable species of birds, plants, and wildflowers.

In 1859, Joel Estes and his son Milton allegedly were the first white men to see the open, forest-rimmed valley that now bears their name (Estes Park). The first time she saw it, in the fall of 1873, Isabella Bird, author of *A Lady's Life in the Rocky Mountains,* commented, "Never, nowhere have I seen anything to equal the view into Estes Park." Enos Mills, a naturalist, writer, and conservationist, was a major force behind the creation of Rocky Mountain National Park, which was dedicated in September 1915.

Guidebooks to the park often list 50 or more hikes, but our goal has been to select a small, varied group, all of which begin on the park's east side. Keep in mind that snow can block trails well into June, so not all destinations will be accessible in the spring. The park's proximity to Denver results in significant overcrowding during the peak summer season.

Be aware that the altitude of Estes Park is 7,522 feet. A few days' acclimation will help make hiking here much easier.

33. Cub Lake

DEGREE OF DIFFICULTY: Moderate
ROUND-TRIP DISTANCE: 4.60 miles
ROUND-TRIP TIME: 3 hours 30 minutes (2 hours up, 1 hour 30 minutes down)
STARTING ALTITUDE: 8,080 feet
ELEVATION GAIN: 540 feet
MAPS: USGS Longs Peak, McHenry's Peak, Rocky Mountain National Park brochure

A favorite hike for families with young children, the Cub Lake Trail exposes the visitor to beaver dams, a profusion of wildflowers, several varieties of trees, and many species of birds. Although the trail winds in and out of the trees, the hike can be very hot unless you start early. It is essential to carry an adequate supply of water. For the novice, the hike is a good introduction to higher trails. Much of the altitude gain occurs in a series of switchbacks near the end of the hike.

Getting There: From the Beaver Meadows Entrance Station, drive 0.2 mile west and turn left onto Bear Lake Road. At 1.3 miles, turn right onto Moraine Park Road. At 1.8 miles, turn left before reaching the Moraine Park Campground. Drive 1.3 miles to the Cub Lake Trailhead. A sign indicates the Cub Lake Trail at the south end of the parking area.

The Hike: Just after the trail begins, cross a bridge adjacent to a beaver pond, where a sign warns of heavy horse traffic. At 0.05 mile, another bridge spans the Big Thompson River. The wide path, rising and dipping, now begins to cross Moraine Park, moving in and out of groves of ponderosa pine and Douglas fir. At 0.50 mile, the trail turns west along the edge of Moraine Park. Here it is bordered by ferns, scrub trees, conifers, and aspen. Several 12,000- to 13,000-foot peaks are visible to the west, often with snow on them. In places, the trail becomes narrow and rocky.

At 0.90 mile, a large pond appears on the left; the trail then passes several smaller ponds. The trail widens at 1.20 miles as it rises gradually through the evergreens. Another large beaver pond is located at 1.60 miles on the left. This is not Cub Lake, as one nine-year-old thought because it was half the size of Bear Lake. At 1.70 miles, the trail begins to climb more steeply through conifer and aspen groves and becomes rockier. Pause along the switchbacks to catch your breath. At 2.20 miles, arrive at the first of two signs

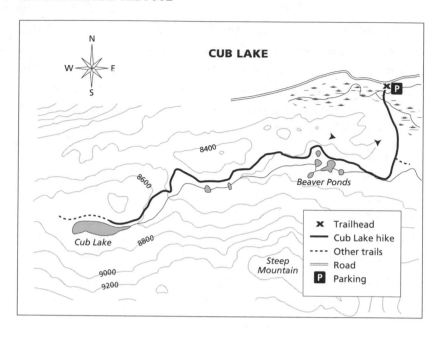

on the left for the Cub Creek Campground. You will reach the lake at 2.30 miles.

The wide, pleasant trail that runs above the north shore of Cub Lake provides many points of lakeside access for rest and picnics. Ducks cruise among the profuse yellow water lilies dotting the lake, whose west end is dominated by Stones Peak (12,922 feet). Retrace your steps to the parking lot.

34. Arch Rocks and The Pool

DEGREE OF DIFFICULTY: Easy
ROUND-TRIP DISTANCE: 3.40 miles
ROUND-TRIP TIME: 2 hours 10 minutes (1 hour 10 minutes up, 1 hour down)
STARTING ALTITUDE: 8,155 feet
ELEVATION GAIN: 245 feet
MAPS: USGS McHenry's Peak, Rocky Mountain National Park brochure

This easy, popular hike is a good conditioner and introduction to Rocky Mountain National Park for the unacclimated older hiker. The elevation gain is modest, the ascents and descents are quite gentle, and the views obtained while driving to the trailhead through Moraine Park are impressive. During summer, go early in the day to beat both the heat and the many families with small children. The hike up a canyon follows the north bank of the Big Thompson River, then crosses a wooden bridge at The Pool. Many short, easy paths lead down to the river's edge and are ideal for picnic and rest stops. Driving back from the hike, stop at the Moraine Park Museum for a worthwhile visit.

Getting There: From the Beaver Meadows Entrance Station, drive 0.2 mile west and turn left onto Bear Lake Road. At 1.3 miles, turn right onto Moraine Park Road. At 1.8 miles, turn left before reaching the Moraine Park Campground. Drive 1.3 more miles to the Cub Lake Trailhead and 0.8 more mile to the parking area at the Fern Lake Trailhead. You will have passed several other parking areas, including one with restrooms, on the way. The last section of road is unpaved.

The Hike: The trail begins on the west side of the parking lot at a sign for The Pool (1.70 miles), Fern Lake (3.80 miles), and Bear Lake (8.50 miles). The path is wide and occasionally rocky as it winds close to, away from, and above the Big Thompson River on the left as you head upstream. At 0.14 mile, the trail runs adjacent to a rockfall from the cliff on the right. At 0.35 mile and again at 0.40 mile, cross a short plank bridge over a stream as the valley widens. At 0.80 mile, pass another rockfall on the right. Note the large

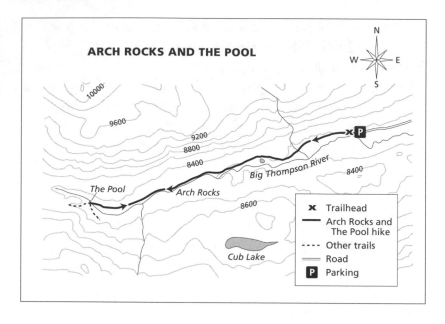

boulders near the river as the path winds under or near aspen, cottonwood, maple, birch, and alder trees.

The trail gradually ascends, and at 1.20 miles huge boulders on either side of the trail appear to form an arch. The trail goes between, or alternatively around, these boulders for 600 feet. At 1.30 miles, a sign points to the Arch Rocks Campground up a trail on the right. At 1.70 miles, you will come to another rockslide. Just beyond it is a bridge over the river, with a small, clear pool beneath it. You may spot water ouzels here. Signs on the far side of the river indicate trails to Fern Lake, Cub Lake, and Mill Creek Basin. To return to the parking area, retrace your steps.

35. Alberta Falls

DEGREE OF DIFFICULTY: Easy
ROUND-TRIP DISTANCE: 1.20 miles
ROUND-TRIP TIME: 40 minutes (25 minutes up, 15 minutes down)
STARTING ALTITUDE: 9,240 feet
ELEVATION GAIN: 160 feet
MAPS: USGS McHenry's Peak, Rocky Mountain National
    Park brochure

This short hike above 9,000 feet is a good conditioner for higher destinations. It is heavily traveled in summer and is often quite sunny and hot. Tree size and density still have not fully recovered from a forest fire that burned the area in 1900. The falls on Glacier Creek were named for Alberta Sprague, wife of an early area resident.

Getting There: From the Beaver Meadows Entrance Station, drive 0.2 mile and turn left onto Bear Lake Road. Proceed 8.7 more miles to the small Glacier Gorge parking lot, where toilets are available. If the lot is full, which it usually is by 8:00 A.M. in summer, use the shuttle bus, available from June to October. To catch the shuttle bus, drive up Bear Lake Road approximately 5.0 miles from the entrance station to a parking lot across from the Glacier Basin Campground. Alternatively, a small parking area might be available 0.26 mile before the Glacier Gorge lot.

The Hike: From the south side of the Glacier Gorge parking lot, cross the road and start up a 120-foot paved trail to the Glacier Gorge Trail signboard, which has a map and park information. From here, a flat, wide dirt trail crosses a bridge over Glacier Creek at 0.03 mile. At 0.05 mile, a sign indicates the Alberta Falls Trail to the right.

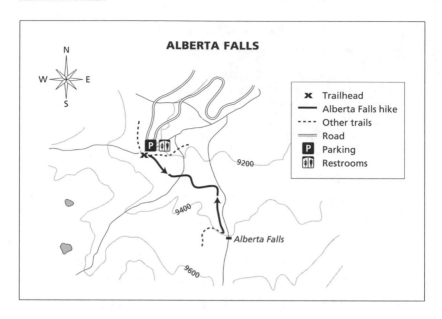

The generally ascending trail passes through a boulder field. The trees here are a mixture of aspen, fir, and spruce. Wildflowers and wild fruits often are found adjacent to the trail, as are birds such as gray and mountain blue jays. Cross bridges at 0.15 and 0.19 mile, before encountering a switchback at 0.26 mile. The trail steepens at 0.32 mile. At 0.40 mile, the gorge's sheer rock sides and torrent of water are clearly visible.

Continue to ascend. A short trail to the right at 0.47 mile leads down to the creek. Continue on the main trail, which at 0.51 mile passes under a canopy of aspen and pine. At 0.53 mile, the stream roars by on the left, just below the trail. A beaver dam upstream has created a small, quiet pool at 0.55 mile. Arrive at the lovely falls at 0.60 mile. This is a fine spot for a picnic or a contemplative rest. When you are ready, retrace your steps to the parking lot.

36. Mills Lake

DEGREE OF DIFFICULTY: Hard
ROUND-TRIP DISTANCE: 4.90 miles
ROUND-TRIP TIME: 3 hours 30 minutes (2 hours up, 1 hour 30 minutes down)
STARTING ALTITUDE: 9,240 feet
ELEVATION GAIN: 700 feet
MAPS: USGS McHenry's Peak, Rocky Mountain National Park brochure

Named for Enos Mills, a naturalist and conservationist who was extremely influential in the development of Rocky Mountain National Park, this beautiful lake is well worth the effort spent getting there. Some consider it the loveliest lake in the park. At 9,940 feet, it is one of the highest destinations we describe. One reason for starting very early in the morning is to experience the spectacular, clear view of the mountains bordering Moraine Park as you drive to the Glacier Gorge parking area. The other reason is that this small parking lot is usually full before 8:00 A.M. in summer. We label this hike a hard one because of the boulders you must scramble over at high altitude near the end of the trail.

Getting There: Follow the directions to the Glacier Gorge parking area given for Alberta Falls (Hike #35).

The Hike: The description of the first 0.60 mile is the same as for the Alberta Falls hike. From the falls, continue to ascend in the pine forest on what is now a narrow and intermittently rockier trail. At 0.92 mile, Glacier Creek roars below on the left. Come upon some stone steps and a switchback at 1.02 miles. A good view of the mountains to the north awaits you at 1.09 miles. The trail heads southeast up a canyon at 1.23 miles and switchbacks to the north-

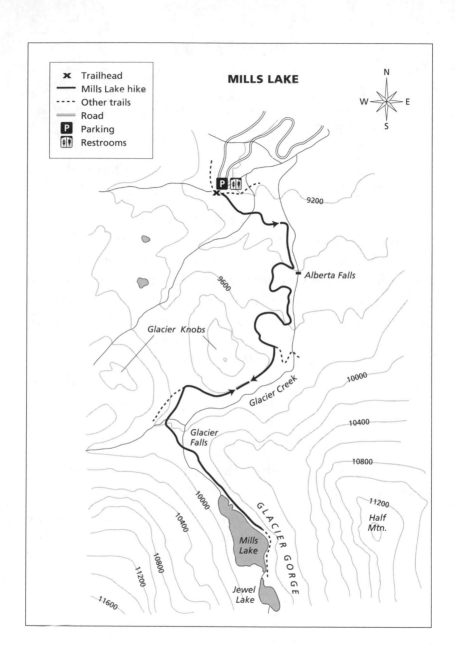

Longs Peak from Mills Lake, Rocky Mountain National Park.

east at 1.29 miles. At 1.40 miles, reach a junction with the North Longs Peak Trail. A sign here (which you should follow) indicates that Mills Lake is 1.10 miles to the right. The views north and west remain impressive.

Continue your ascent up the canyon and at 1.57 miles cross a talus field with a steep dropoff to the left. For those unfamiliar with the word, talus refers to a slope consisting of material fallen from the face of a cliff above. The scree (a loose mass of rock) ends at 1.64 miles, where the trail becomes easier. Switchback at 1.79 miles, after which the trail descends steeply for a bit. Re-enter the forest. At 1.88 miles, a sign indicates that the Glacier Gorge Junction is 1.90 miles behind you. Turn left at a larger sign just beyond that indicates Mills Lake is 0.60 mile farther. Descend slightly on a wide trail through denser evergreens, then ascend to a hitching rack at 1.99 miles, beyond which no horses are allowed.

Cross a plank bridge over Icy Brook at 2.02 miles. Continue through a rock- and boulder-strewn area, after which the trail disappears as the route heads over boulders. Happily, frequent cairns mark the way. It is worth looking back at the cairns to get a sense of their placement for the descent. Limber pines emerge from rocky cracks. The trail reappears briefly at 2.13 miles, after which cairns again mark the way. At 2.18 miles, cross a two-part plank bridge over Glacier Creek and head right. You will encounter log steps at 2.22 miles, before moving back into the boulders, where the trail is marked by cairns.

At 2.25 miles the trail resumes and the lake is visible, with the creek pouring out of it. Continue following the cairns to the north shore of the lake at 2.45 miles. The outlet is clogged with fallen trees. Look south across this lovely lake at Longs Peak (14,255 feet) and Pagoda Peak (13,497 feet). There is a short trail on the east side of the lake that allows you to get out onto boulders in the lake for a more extensive view. When ready, retrace your steps back to the parking lot. It somehow seems easier to follow the cairns downhill.

37. Bierstadt Lake

DEGREE OF DIFFICULTY: Moderate
ROUND-TRIP DISTANCE: 4.22 miles
ROUND-TRIP TIME: 3 hours (1 hour 30 minutes up, 1 hour 30 minutes down)
STARTING ALTITUDE: 9,475 feet
ELEVATION GAIN: Although Bierstadt Lake is 59 feet below the starting point at Bear Lake, two Rocky Mountain Park brochures list the gain for this hike as 245 feet (probably from Bear Lake) and 566 feet (probably from the Bierstadt Lake Trailhead). Take your pick!
MAPS: USGS McHenry's Peak, Rocky Mountain National Park brochure

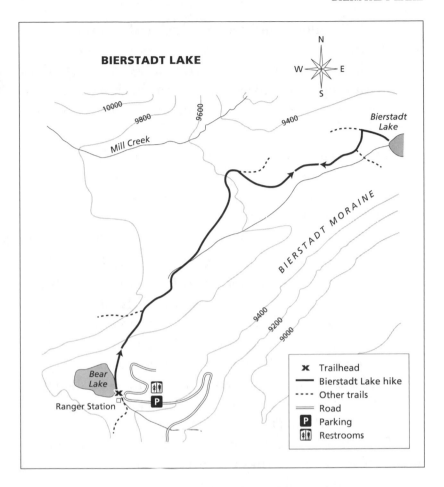

This lake is named for artist Albert Bierstadt, who painted so many impressive views of this area in the 1870s. The trail, entirely within a conifer forest, offers a sense of isolation in the wilderness and takes you to a pristine, beautiful high mountain lake. The hike can be done either round-trip from Bear Lake, from Bear Lake to Bierstadt Lake and then on to the Bierstadt Lake Trailhead (a distance of 3.42 miles, almost all of which is downhill), or as a loop up and back from the Bierstadt Lake Trailhead.

How high is Bierstadt Lake? One Rocky Mountain Park hiking trails brochure gives the lake's altitude as 8,850 feet; another gives it as 9,416 feet. USGS maps record it as 9,416 feet.

Getting There: From the Beaver Meadows Entrance Station, drive 0.2 mile and turn left onto Bear Lake Road. Drive 9.6 more miles to the Bear Lake parking area. A staffed ranger station is located there, offering maps and information. There also are toilet facilities and a shuttle-bus stop.

The Hike: From the edge of the parking lot, walk toward Bear Lake. The trail forks at 0.04 mile. Go right. At 0.14 mile, a sign indicates that Bierstadt Lake again is to the right, 2.00 miles away. The wide, well-maintained trail ascends steeply through conifers and aspen along the south side of the Bierstadt Moraine. At 0.49 mile, another sign at a fork indicates Bierstadt Lake is 1.70 miles to the right. The trail now narrows, becomes rockier, and ascends farther. Hallett Peak (12,713 feet) and Flattop Mountain (12,324 feet) are visible through the trees. The orange markers, high on the trees, that guide skiers and snowshoers in winter are helpful for hikers, too.

Arrive at the hike's high point at 0.65 mile. A long, gradual descent, steep initially but then flatter, leads to a sign at 1.24 miles indicating that Bierstadt Lake is 1.00 mile farther to the right. Continue right and descend gradually. At 1.81 miles, come to a small meadow. At its end, another sign at a fork indicates that you can take the trail either right or left around the lake and that the Bierstadt Lake Trailhead is 1.30 miles to the right. Go right. At 2.00

miles, another sign indicates that a trail around the lake can be accessed either by going left or by retracing your steps, that the Bierstadt Lake Trailhead is 1.20 miles straight ahead, and that Bear Lake is 1.90 miles behind you. Turn left and descend toward the lake to a hitching rack at 2.09 miles. At a "No horses beyond this point" sign, you will see the lake, which you come to at 2.11 miles. The shore is bordered by marsh grass. On one of our hikes to this lake, we came upon a moose having breakfast on the shore, ducks diving in the 7.4-acre lake, and lovely mountain jays begging for food. A trail circles the lake, and Longs Peak can be seen from the northwest shore. Return to Bear Lake by retracing your steps.

For an easier hike, instead of returning to Bear Lake, hike down to the Bierstadt Lake Trailhead. To do this, head back to the sign indicating that the trailhead is 1.20 miles away. Turn left and descend via several switchbacks to the trailhead. The total distance for this hike is 3.42 miles. The shuttle waiting area is a few feet down the road. The shuttle will return you to the Bear Lake parking area if you did not park at the trailhead.

From the Bierstadt Lake Trailhead, the round-trip distance to and from the lake is 2.60 miles, starting at 8,870 feet and ascending to 9,430 feet.

38. Nymph Lake

DEGREE OF DIFFICULTY: Easy
ROUND-TRIP DISTANCE: 1.00 mile
ROUND-TRIP TIME: 35 minutes (20 minutes up, 15 minutes down)
STARTING ALTITUDE: 9,475 feet
ELEVATION GAIN: 225 feet
MAPS: USGS McHenry's Peak, Rocky Mountain National Park brochure

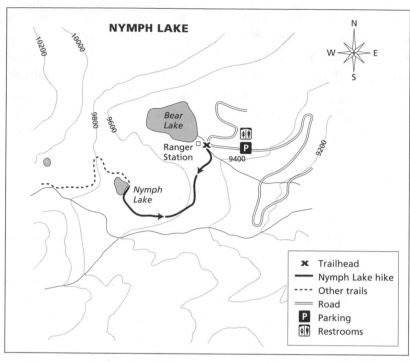

NYMPH LAKE

Bear
Lake

Ranger
Station

Nymph
Lake

10200
10000
9800
9600
9400
9200

N
W E
S

✖ Trailhead
━ Nymph Lake hike
╴╴╴ Other trails
══ Road
🅿 Parking
🚻 Restrooms

Nymph Lake, Rocky Mountain National Park.

This is one of the park's most beautiful and heavily visited lakes. If, however, you start before 8:00 A.M., the trail is often uncrowded, even in summer. Parking is usually available at Bear Lake.

Getting There: Follow the directions given for Bierstadt Lake (Hike #37).

The Hike: Start at the ranger station. A sign 200 feet beyond indicates that Nymph, Dream, and Emerald Lakes are to the left. The trail, wide and partially paved due to heavy foot traffic, ascends moderately steeply through fir, spruce, and pine. To the left, note the good views of the mountains. Nymph Lake, which you will reach at 0.50 mile, has many yellow pond lilies floating on its surface. Hallett Peak (12,713 feet) dominates the skyline. The trail runs along the shore, reaching the western edge after an additional 0.10 mile. Retrace your steps to the parking lot.

39. Dream Lake

DEGREE OF DIFFICULTY: Easy
ROUND-TRIP DISTANCE: 1.14 miles from Nymph Lake; 2.14 miles from Bear Lake
ROUND-TRIP TIME: 1 hour 5 minutes (40 minutes up from Nymph Lake, 25 minutes down); 1 hour 40 minutes (1 hour up from Bear Lake, 40 minutes down)
STARTING ALTITUDE: 9,700 feet at Nymph Lake; 9,475 feet at Bear Lake
ELEVATION GAIN: 200 feet from Nymph Lake; 425 feet from Bear Lake
MAPS: USGS McHenry's Peak, Rocky Mountain National Park brochure

Lovely Dream Lake, a bit farther up the trail, also attracts many visitors. Again, if you start before 8:00 A.M., the trail should be uncrowded.

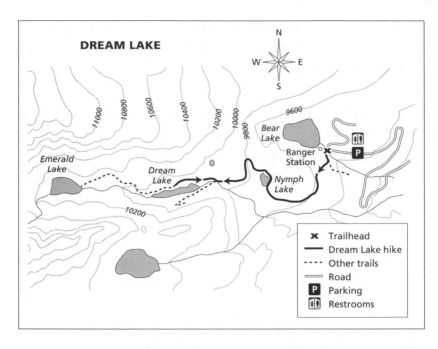

DREAM LAKE

11000 · 10800 · 10600 · 10400 · 10200 · 10000 · 9800 · 9600 · 10200

Bear Lake

Emerald Lake

Dream Lake

Nymph Lake

Ranger Station

✖	Trailhead
—	Dream Lake hike
---	Other trails
═	Road
🅿	Parking
🚻	Restrooms

Longs Peak from Dream Lake, Rocky Mountain National Park.

Getting There: Follow the directions given for Bierstadt Lake (Hike #37).

The Hike: From Nymph Lake, the dirt trail ascends moderately. At 0.70 mile (measured from the trailhead at Bear Lake), pass a large rock outcropping on the right. At 0.80 mile, there is a lovely view of Nymph Lake to the left and Longs Peak (14,255 feet) to the south. At 0.90 mile, Tyndall Creek rushes by below on the left; a bit farther on, the trail runs immediately adjacent to it.

The trail now becomes steeper until you reach a wooden bridge at about 1.00 mile. Continue to hike west, with Hallett Peak directly in front of you. A sign at 1.01 miles indicates Dream Lake and Emerald Lake are 0.10 and 0.70 mile ahead, respectively. Cross a plank bridge over a stream at 1.02 miles. At 1.06 miles, another sign indicates that Dream Lake is 50 feet to the left, and Emerald Lake is still 0.70 mile away. A smooth path with many attractive picnic and rest spots runs along the north side of Dream Lake. Retrace your steps to the parking lot.

40. Emerald Lake

DEGREE OF DIFFICULTY: Moderate
ROUND-TRIP DISTANCE: 1.40 miles from Dream Lake; 3.56 miles from Bear Lake
ROUND-TRIP TIME: 1 hour 35 minutes (1 hour up from Dream Lake, 35 minutes down); 3 hours 15 minutes (2 hours up from Bear Lake, 1 hour 15 minutes down)
STARTING ALTITUDE: 9,900 feet at Dream Lake; 9,475 feet at Bear Lake
ELEVATION GAIN: 180 feet from Dream Lake; 605 feet from Bear Lake
Maps: USGS McHenry's Peak, Rocky Mountain National Park brochure

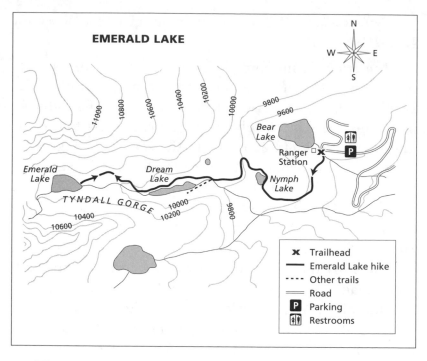

The same advice applies as for Nymph Lake and Dream Lake.

Getting There: Follow the directions given to Bierstadt Lake (Hike #37).

The Hike: The hike to Emerald Lake is more strenuous than to the other two lakes. The trail from Dream Lake ascends for approximately 0.50 mile along a steep, rocky path under evergreens along Tyndall Creek and requires careful attention to footing. Cross a plank bridge. At 0.60 mile, the trail flattens out a bit and descends slightly to the lake. Water gushes into the lake from impressive Hallett Peak, where mountain climbers can often be seen. Retrace your steps to the parking lot.

Aspen

A frequent destination for the world's rich and famous, Aspen offers a variety of wonderful hiking experiences for the older hiker. We have been exploring trails here since 1954, when we stayed in a cabin for $1.50 a night. Things do change!

Prospecting began in 1878. By 1887, Aspen was a roaring mining camp of 15,000 people, many of whom were engaged in extracting silver, lead, and other valuable ores from Aspen Mountain to the south and Smuggler Mountain to the east. The collapse of silver prices in the 1890s nearly turned Aspen into a ghost town. By 1941, it had only 705 residents. The development of the ski industry and promotion of cultural events such as the Aspen Music Festival, which takes place every summer, now attract tens of thousands of visitors annually. The year-round population in the 2000 census was 5,914.

There are many trails in the Aspen area, ranging from short, easy hikes to arduous climbs up several of Colorado's "fourteeners." Some of the hikes that we enjoyed decades ago, such as Buckskin Pass and the entire Lost Man Loop, are beyond us now, but many others are still achievable and satisfying. We have deliberately chosen to describe hikes of only easy to moderate difficulty, in hopes of enticing visitors to explore the natural beauty of the Colorado mountains. Remember that Aspen sits at an altitude of 7,908 feet; lowlanders should allow several days to acclimate before going up into the mountains. For conditioning, we detail an east-side city walk. Similar hikes can be taken through the business district and the west side. We have omitted the Ute Trail, which is commonly suggested for visitors, because it gains about 1,700 feet in just over a mile and is so steep in places as to be quite treacherous for older folks. As the pianist Yefim Bronfman said at the start of a 1999 concert, "I now know what they mean when they say to performers, 'Break a leg.'" He did just that on the Ute Trail.

At the Forest Service Aspen Ranger District headquarters (806 West Hallam Street), information about terrain and weather, flora and fauna books, trail guides, and brief handouts describing the hikes are available.

41. The Rio Grande Trail

DEGREE OF DIFFICULTY: Easy
ROUND-TRIP DISTANCE: 2.62 miles
ROUND-TRIP TIME: 1 hour 20 minutes
STARTING ALTITUDE: 7,700 feet
Elevation Loss: 100 feet
Maps: Aspen City map, USGS Aspen

This trail includes both paved and unpaved portions. We suggest avoiding the paved portion (starting at Mill and Puppy Smith Streets), which is full of rollerbladers, bikers, and runners. The unpaved trail runs along what was once the right-of-way for the Denver and Rio Grande Railroad, going west toward Woody Creek.

Getting There: Drive west on Main Street (Colorado Highway 82) from its intersection with Mill Street for 1.0 mile to the stoplight at Cemetery Lane. Turn right, travel 1.2 miles (crossing the Slaughterhouse Bridge), and turn left into a parking area at Harry Stein Park. A short paved road leads west out of the park.

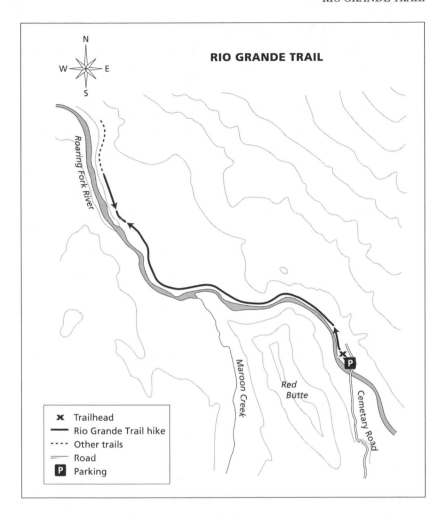

The Hike: The paved trail to the west (right) gives way in 120 feet to an unpaved, wide gravel road that parallels the Roaring Fork River on the left. It descends gently through aspen, cottonwoods, evergreens, and box elders. The beautiful river really roars at times as you move into a canyon at 0.42 mile. A large rock overhang looms on the right. At 0.61 mile, arrive at a sizable pond on the right, frequented by ducks. White-water rapids roil in the river.

The trail ascends slightly, and at 0.72 mile Maroon Creek, on the left, enters the Roaring Fork River. At 0.91 mile, the canyon opens up, and at 1.06 miles there is a trail on the left that leads down to the river. Continue on the road, which is now high above the river. At 1.30 miles, several waterfalls cascade down the cliff faces on the right. On the left, the Aspen Metro Sanitation District plant sits adjacent to the river. The back of the Airport Business Center is also visible on top of a bluff. At 1.31 miles, there is a nice view down the Roaring Fork Valley. We turn around here, as the trail beyond does not offer much more of scenic interest.

42. Aspen City Walk

DEGREE OF DIFFICULTY: Easy
ROUND-TRIP DISTANCE: 2.85 miles
ROUND-TRIP TIME: 1 hour 25 minutes
STARTING ALTITUDE: 7,900 feet
ELEVATION GAIN: Approximately 100 feet
MAP: Aspen City Map (from Chamber of Commerce)

Getting There: Parking in Aspen can be difficult and expensive, particularly during the week, so we suggest driving 0.7 mile from the junction of Mill and Main Streets to Glory Hole Park, a small, quiet oasis with a pond, trees, and benches at Original Street and Ute Avenue. On-street two-hour parking between 8:00 A.M. and 6:00 P.M. is usually available. Additional parking can be found on Queen Street, just off Neale Avenue.

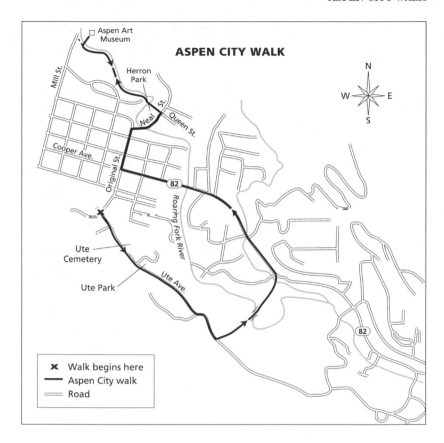

The Hike: At the corner of Original Street and Ute Avenue, there is a sign identifying the Ute Avenue Trail. Go east from here, pass the unmarked Ute Cemetery on the left, which in 1999 was overgrown with native grasses, and at 0.40 mile pass the entrance to Ute Park. Continue on the paved street. At 0.60 mile, the Roaring Fork River appears on the left. At 0.70 mile, pass a bridge on the left and continue to the second bridge over the river. As you cross it, look east for a good view up toward Independence Pass.

At 0.80 mile, continue straight while passing entrances to private driveways on either side. Just beyond them, there is a small pond on the left. From here you have a nice view of Red Mountain. Cross a bridge and go left to Colorado Highway 82. Walk west on the highway shoulder into town, past beautiful flowers at the entrance to the Aspen Club at 0.90 mile. The highway shortly becomes Cooper Avenue. You will come to a sidewalk at 1.20 miles and cross the Roaring Fork River soon after. At the intersection of Cooper Avenue and Original Street (1.40 miles), turn right (north) and walk to Neal Street (1.60 miles). Turn right on Neal Street, cross the No Problem Bridge, and walk to Queen Street before turning left to enter Herron Park on the paved Rio Grande Trail.

This restful spot has picnic areas, benches, a sandy area adjacent to a wading pool for children, swings, and toilet facilities. It makes a nice lunch or snack stop. Exit the park on its west side via another bridge over the river at 1.65 miles. Only fly-fishing is allowed on this portion of the river, where catch-and-release rules prevail. At 1.70 miles, pass a sign pointing right to Oklahoma Flats (stay to the left). Pass Newberry Park on the left before reaching the Aspen Theater in the Park at 1.90 miles. Continue on over a railroad trestle spanning the Roaring Fork River. A 150-foot trail to the left leads to the river, just opposite Mill Street, where you may choose to end your hike. Or, if you desire, you can stay on the path and at 2.10 miles reach the Aspen Art Museum. Just beyond it is a small pond for breeding cutthroat trout.

Retrace your steps through Herron Park to Neal Street and then south up Original Street to Glory Hole Park.

43. Hunter Valley Trail

DEGREE OF DIFFICULTY: Easy
ROUND-TRIP DISTANCE: 2.82 miles
ROUND-TRIP TIME: 1 hour 30 minutes
STARTING ALTITUDE: 8,350 feet
ELEVATION GAIN: Approximately 425 feet
MAP: USGS Aspen

This trail is one of our favorites. We probably first hiked it in the mid-1950s, starting at the Hunter Creek Trailhead on what is now Lone Pine Road, about a half mile from North Mill and Main Streets. We never enjoyed the first part of this hike, which runs steeply through the woods next to Hunter Creek, as much as the second part, where the Hunter Valley opens out, offering wide vistas. Eventually, after considerable dispute between the Forest Service and private landowners, easier access to Hunter Valley was made available. The valley is full of wildflowers in the spring and early summer, and old abandoned cabins along the way provide a sense of history.

Note that county signs refer to the trail as the Hunter Creek Trail, whereas Forest Service signs call it the Hunter Valley Trail.

Getting There: From its intersection with Main Street, drive north on N. Mill Street, cross the Roaring Fork River, and bear left onto the winding Red Mountain Road. Bear sharply right at a sign that says 10 MPH, and at 1.5 miles from your starting point, turn right onto Hunter Creek Road at a sign that says "Hunter Creek Trailhead Parking." After 0.2 mile more, turn left at a similar sign just before two stone pillars with a "Private" sign. A right turn after 0.1 more mile takes you to the dirt parking area.

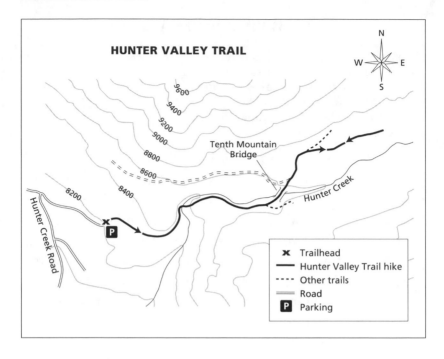

The Hike: Walk back to the entrance to the parking area, past a wooden building to a trail sign that says "Hunter Creek Trail—Steep Access. For easier winter access, walk road ¼ mile to where Hunter Creek Trail crosses Hunter Creek Road." We follow this advice in the summer, too. Walk down the road to the stone pillars, turn left, and walk up the private road. Pedestrian access is permitted, according to Forest Service personnel. It is likely that you will be impressed with many of the private homes that cling precariously to the cliff sides.

At 0.31 mile, there is a sign on the right for the Hunter Creek Trail. Just beyond, you can see where the dirt trail from the parking lot reaches the road. Start hiking on the

Hunter Creek, Aspen.

Abandoned building, Hunter Valley, Aspen.

Hunter Creek Trail, which ascends gently, though the terrain is somewhat rocky. A regulations sign is posted at 0.35 mile. At 0.44 mile, cross the Benedict Bridge over Hunter Creek. Ignore a trail just to the right that leads down to the lower Hunter Creek Trail access. The trail now ascends moderately steeply in the drainage between Red Mountain and Smuggler Mountain.

At 0.47 mile, a trail on the right heads over to Smuggler Mountain. Ignore this and ascend up an old road, from which several short spurs lead to Hunter Creek on the left. At 0.71 mile, the trail levels out a bit and continues to climb through aspen and evergreens. At 0.88 mile, cross a new road at a truck crossing sign. You will come to a White

River National Forest boundary sign at 1.05 miles. As you enter a meadow, the trail is fairly level.

At 1.28 miles, turn left at the Hunter Valley Trail #1992 sign and cross the Tenth Mountain Bridge over Hunter Creek. There is a moderate ascent to a fork and signboard at 1.33 miles. Go right and head northeast on an old road past four wooden houses in various states of collapse. Another sign at 1.41 miles indicates the Hunter Valley Trail. You can end the hike here and return to the parking lot by retracing your steps. If you wish to go farther, the trail, with good views of the Elk Mountain Range, will continue its gradual ascent for approximately 2.50 miles to Van Horn Park; 7.00 more miles will take you to the site of the old town of Lenado and the Midway Pass Trail.

44. Weller Lake Trail

DEGREE OF DIFFICULTY: Easy
ROUND-TRIP DISTANCE: 1.40 miles
ROUND-TRIP TIME: 55 minutes
STARTING ALTITUDE: 9,300 feet
ELEVATION GAIN: 300 feet
MAP: USGS New York Peak

This is a good introductory hike for those not fully adjusted to moderate mountain altitudes. The lake, situated in a bowl at the base of New York and Difficult Peaks, is reached after a steady climb through aspen and spruce in the White River National Forest east of Aspen. Despite the lack of a well-defined trail around the lake, it is not too difficult to scramble at least partway around.

Getting There: From its intersection with Mill Street, drive east on Main Street (Colorado Highway 82) toward Independence Pass for 8.6 miles. Don't park in the turnoff

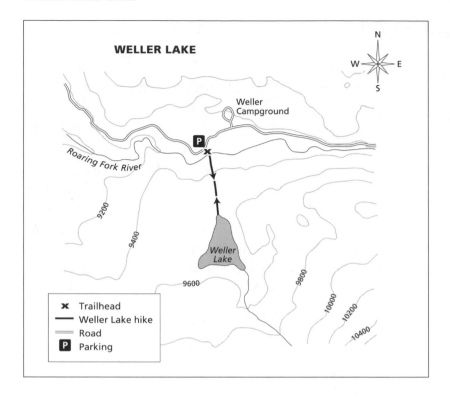

opposite the Weller Campground entrance but go a few feet beyond to a parking area on the right for the Weller Lake Trailhead. The trail begins at the lot's east end.

The Hike: Descend a few wooden steps to the trail, which forks almost immediately. Go right along the Roaring Fork River. The narrow trail, which may be muddy and overgrown, veers slightly away from the river and then back again. At 0.16 mile, cross a bridge, walk up 10 steps, and note a sign at 0.19 mile pointing to a Roaring Fork overlook on the left. To reach it, go about 230 feet, crossing two

Weller Lake, Aspen.

bridges. To resume the hike, return to the overlook sign and head right, toward Weller Lake.

The trail now ascends more steeply, crosses a stream at 0.30 mile, and at 0.32 mile reaches a sign for the Collegiate Peaks Wilderness/White River National Forest. The rocky path now ascends through the forest via switchbacks at 0.35, 0.40, 0.45, 0.48, and 0.53 mile. At 0.56 mile, a bridge crosses the torrent of water rushing out of Weller Lake. There is a great deal of timber deadfall adjacent to the lake, but the walk here is quite pleasant. At 0.70 mile, reach the shore of the lake, whose drainage is clogged with dead trees and branches. Fish often are seen jumping in Weller Lake, which offers a good view of the surrounding peaks.

45. Maroon Lake Scenic Trail

DEGREE OF DIFFICULTY: Easy
ROUND-TRIP DISTANCE: 1.18 miles
ROUND-TRIP TIME: 45 minutes
STARTING ALTITUDE: 9,580 feet
ELEVATION GAIN: Negligible
MAP: USGS Maroon Bells

The trails around Maroon Lake and Crater Lake are among the most popular and heavily used in the Aspen area because of the spectacular views they offer of the Maroon Bells (both over 14,000 feet), which indeed resemble two red bells. For this reason, the Forest Service has limited automobile access, and from mid-June through September, Maroon Creek Road is closed from 8:30 A.M. to 5:00 P.M. Shuttle buses to Maroon Lake are available at Rubey Park (E. Durant Street between S. Mill and S. Galena Streets) in Aspen. Tickets are moderately priced. Bus schedules can be obtained at most lodgings, or by calling the Roaring

Fork Transit Agency at (970) 925-8484. You can drive up to Maroon Lake before 8:30 A.M. and come down at any time during the day.

Getting There: Drive west on Main Street (Colorado Highway 82) from its junction with Mill Street for 1.2 miles. Turn left onto Maroon Creek Road, keep right, and drive 9.8 more miles to the Maroon Lake parking lots. Park in the Day Use area. The trail begins near toilets at a signboard with a map and information about the local flora and fauna.

The Hike: At a fork approximately 350 feet from the start of the trail, go left along the shore of the lake on a wide trail. At 0.16 mile, the trail is joined by the right fork, and at 0.27 mile there is a sign describing the Deadly Bells and their climbing hazards. Falls from their crumbling rock faces have caused a tragic number of deaths. In 1965–1966, seven climbers died in a nine-month period. Continue to the left, but take time to look down the valley and up at the mountains. At 0.38 mile, there is a beaver dam at the end of the lake. At 0.43 mile, cross a stream on a small plank bridge and continue on a wide gravel-and-dirt path. Ignore a small path to the right at 0.47 mile.

At 0.50 mile, cross another bridge over the creek inlet to the lake. Just beyond, there is a trail off to the right that we do not advise taking because it ascends very steeply to join the Crater Lake Trail. Continue straight and enter an area of evergreens at 0.59 mile where there is a large rockfall. The trail becomes invisible at this point, and we advise turning back and retracing your steps. Just before you reach the signboard at the trailhead, note a trail on your right crossing a bridge over the outflow of the lake. This is

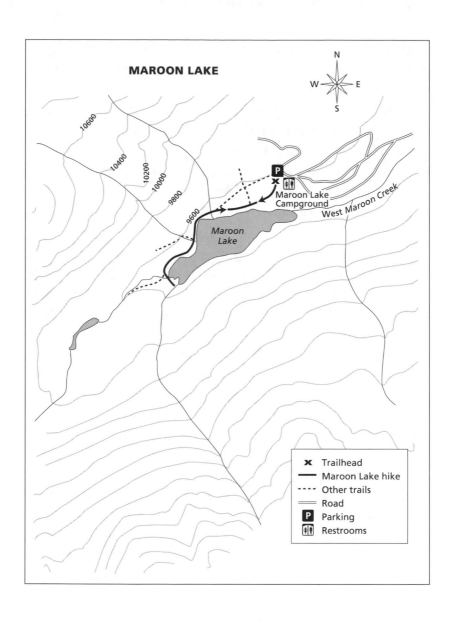

the start of the Maroon Creek Trail, which follows the creek down into the valley. If you decide to take this trail, remember that you have to come back up.

46. Crater Lake

DEGREE OF DIFFICULTY: Moderate
ROUND-TRIP DISTANCE: 3.64 miles
ROUND-TRIP TIME: 2 hours 55 minutes (1 hour 40 minutes up, 1 hour 15 minutes down)
STARTING ALTITUDE: 9,580 feet
ELEVATION GAIN: 596 feet
MAP: USGS Maroon Bells

This hike takes you up into the Maroon Bells–Snowmass Wilderness. No dogs are allowed at Crater Lake unless they are passing through, and at all times they must be on a leash. Camping is allowed only at designated sites, and only stoves, not open fires, are permitted within 0.5 mile of the lake. The lake is fed largely by runoff from the Bells—Maroon Peak (14,156 feet) and North Maroon Peak (14,014 feet).

Although considerable effort may be required to reach the 10,076-foot-high lake, the glorious views of the Bells, Pyramid Peak (14,018 feet), and Crater Lake itself are well worth it.

Getting There: Follow the directions given for the Maroon Lake Scenic Trail (Hike #45).

The Hike: Begin at the signboard at the start of the Maroon Lake Scenic Trail and walk 350 feet to Maroon Lake. Bear right around the lakeshore and at a sign at 0.28 mile, take the right fork toward Crater Lake. The left fork goes there, too, but it is steeper and rockier than the one we suggest. The narrow trail ascends gradually, and at 0.42

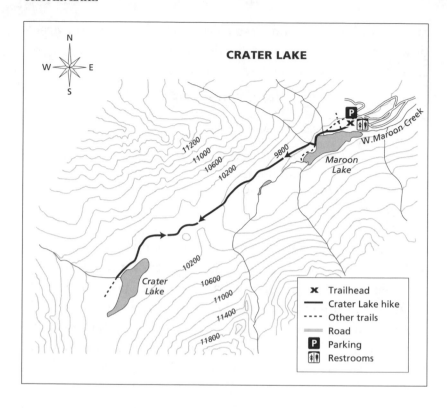

mile you will cross two streams on two wooden bridges. You are now well into aspen, though soon Douglas fir will predominate. At 0.45 mile, there is a sign indicating the Maroon Lake Scenic Trail and the beaver pond to the left. Stay right on the Maroon-Snowmass Trail indicated by a sign for the Maroon Bells–Snowmass Wilderness/White River National Forest.

The trail now climbs steeply and at 0.89 mile crosses a talus field in a rockslide area. At 0.98 mile, a sign points right for the Crater Lake Trail (Maroon-Snowmass Trail); the trail to the left goes back to Maroon Lake. The path now becomes steeper and rockier and passes by a rock wall to the right. At 1.17 miles, there is a switchback, and another talus field must be negotiated. Marmots frequently sun themselves on the rocks, and pikas run around squeaking. The trail descends a bit at 1.24 miles, still in talus, then ascends until it regains the dirt track.

Early in the season, columbine and other wildflowers bloom in rocky crevices. At 1.59 miles, the trail peaks and then begins its descent to the lake, first visible at 1.63 miles. A signboard at 1.73 miles notes that the Maroon-Snowmass Trail continues to the right for 3.00 miles to Buckskin Pass, and the West Maroon Trail goes to the left. Head left down to the lake, which you will reach at 1.82 miles. There is an easy trail around the lake, with many spots suitable for a snack or rest stop. The view of the Maroon Bells is spectacular. Pyramid Peak to the southeast adds to the grandeur. When ready, retrace your steps with care to the parking lot.

47. Lost Man Creek Trail

> DEGREE OF DIFFICULTY: Moderate
> ROUND-TRIP DISTANCE: 5.38 miles
> ROUND-TRIP TIME: 3 hours 45 minutes (2 hours 10 minutes up,
>   1 hour 35 minutes down)
> STARTING ALTITUDE: 10,507 feet
> ELEVATION GAIN: 500 feet
> Maps: USGS Mt. Champion, USGS Independence Pass

Most guidebooks describe the entire Lost Man Loop Trail; we cover only the lower third. The loop, which begins near the last switchback going up to Independence Pass on Colorado Highway 82, is nearly 9 miles in length and takes most middle-aged hikers at least 6–8 hours to complete. Older hikers might well take longer. The loop begins at 11,506 feet and ascends to a saddle at 12,800 feet in just under 3 miles. For those able to accomplish this first

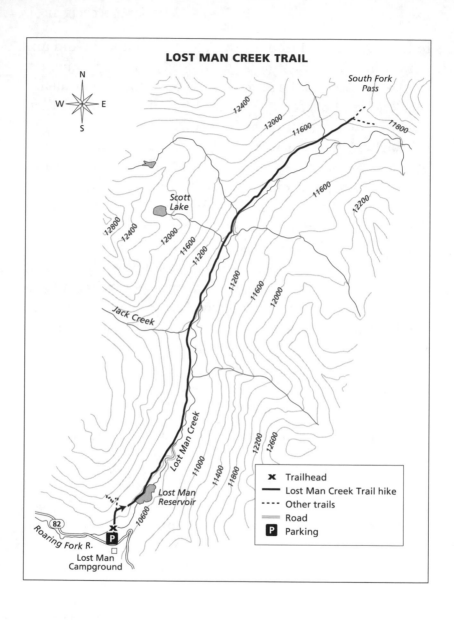

LOST MAN CREEK TRAIL

South Fork Pass

12400
12000
11600
11800

11600

12200

Scott Lake

12800
12400
12000
11600
11200

11200
11600
12000

Jack Creek

12000
12200
12600

Lost Man Creek

11000
11400
11800

10600

Lost Man Reservoir

x Trailhead
— Lost Man Creek Trail hike
- - - Other trails
═ Road
P Parking

82

Roaring Fork R.

P

Lost Man Campground

portion, which crosses the Roaring Fork River and passes Independence Lake (the source of the river) and Lost Man Lake (the origin of Lost Man Creek), the views are magnificent. The trail continues down the Lost Man Creek Valley, past the Lost Man Reservoir, to Highway 82 about 4 miles down from the start.

The hike we describe goes up the Lost Man Creek Valley for nearly 3 miles. In our experience, the trail is not heavily used. We have seen deer frequently and elk occasionally, as well as a great variety of birds. The trail, within the Hunter/Frying Pan Wilderness, is usually free of snow by July, but some marshy areas may persist a bit longer.

Getting There: From its intersection with Mill Street, drive east on Main Street (Colorado Highway 82) for 14.5 miles, past highway mile marker 55 on the right, to a parking area opposite the Lost Man Campground.

The Hike: The trailhead is marked by a sign indicating the Lost Man Trail and the Midway Trail to the left, and the Lost Man Reservoir to the right. After filling out the wilderness register, go left on a narrow trail and at 0.10 mile cross a bridge over a stream. The trail, now slightly wider, ascends gently through the evergreen forest to a fork at 0.28 mile. You can take either path; we generally stay left. The ascent is now steeper. At 0.35 mile, pass a sign indicating the Midway Trail to the left. Continue straight. At 0.45 mile, the trail is joined by the right fork bypassed earlier. Reach the Lost Man Reservoir at 0.54 mile. Pass several small trails that lead down to the water.

The valley now widens as you climb to the northeast, heading upstream with Lost Man Creek to your right. You

Lost Man Creek, Aspen.

will come to the wilderness boundary at 0.84 mile. Take time to observe the surrounding mountain peaks, willows, and wildflowers. Continue your ascent on a 2-foot-wide, slightly rocky dirt trail. The creek, noisy at times, is strewn with boulders as it rushes down the valley floor.

After the first mile, the valley narrows. At 1.16 miles, cross a small stream. The ascent is now steeper, and by 1.35 miles the trail runs close to the evergreen forest on the left. A gradual descent approaches the creek at 1.50 miles, then there is a gradual ascent again among trees along the slightly rocky path. At 1.60 miles, leave the trees, re-entering them at 1.65 miles. The trail is now wide and easy. At 1.85 miles, pass many fallen logs on your way to a larger stream (Jack Creek) at 1.88 miles. This stream can be crossed either on a log bridge or over stones in the water. Another smaller stream must be crossed on stones. At 1.92 miles, enter a meadow before heading back into the trees again at 1.97 miles.

At 2.21 miles, break out again into the open, reaching a high point above the creek at 2.35 miles. For a time, the trail rises and dips. Cross another small stream at 2.36 miles. Beyond this, the trail climbs more steeply. At 2.42 miles, a 70-foot path to the right leads to an overlook. From here, watch the creek tumbling down over rocks. Regain the main trail, cross yet another small stream, and ascend steeply. Several more streams are forded easily. At 2.61 miles, the trail has been built up over a marshy area.

The valley now narrows. We usually stop at 2.69 miles in a wide area where we have lunch while admiring this beautiful valley. On occasion, we have continued about a mile farther to a trail that goes over South Fork Pass. The time and effort this entails do not provide anything new in the way of scenic views. When ready, retrace your steps to the parking area.

Vail

Construction of Vail began in 1962. Approximately five years earlier, its potential as a ski area had been recognized by Peter Seibert and several other veterans of the Tenth Mountain Division, who had trained in the area during World War II. Venture capital initially was difficult to acquire, but eventually the site for Vail Village was purchased for $110 per acre. From the start, growth, including that of Beaver Creek to the west, has been spectacular.

Vail is not only a world-class ski destination but a warm-weather resort as well. Summer activities now rival those in Aspen. A major reason for this warm-weather popularity is the beauty of the adjacent Gore Range. Sir St. George Gore, an Irish baronet whose name is attached also to a mountain, a pass, a creek, and a wilderness area, traveled to what is now Colorado in 1854 on a shooting expedition guided by mountain man Jim Bridger. In three years, he allegedly killed more than 2,000 buffalo, 1,600 elk and deer, and 100 bears in Colorado, Wyoming, and Montana.

We have been hiking in the Vail area since 1980, almost always when the aspen leaves turn to gold. Many of the hikes in this vicinity begin with a steep ascent and are quite long in comparison with others in this book. Consequently, we describe only a few from the many we have done, those we feel are appropriate for older hikers.

48. Vail City Walk

DEGREE OF DIFFICULTY: Easy
ROUND-TRIP DISTANCE: 3.18 miles
ROUND-TRIP TIME: 1 hour 45 minutes
STARTING ALTITUDE: 8,150 feet
ELEVATION GAIN: Negligible
MAP: Vail Walking Map

This is a good way to acclimate to the 8,150-foot altitude and orient yourself to Vail and Lionshead. The walk will take you to the Betty Ford Alpine Gardens and the public library, both well worth an extended visit. The gardens have several ponds and waterfalls that enhance the beauty of its three major divisions—an alpine garden with more than

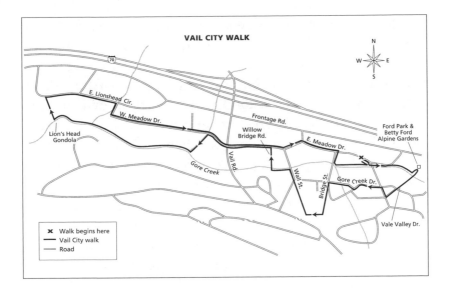

500 varieties of alpine and subalpine flowers and plants, a perennial garden with more than 1,500 varieties, and a meditation garden. The library, built in 1972, won several design awards for its architect. One of the nicest aspects of this walk is that the mountains and the ski slopes are constantly visible. Not on the walk but definitely worth a separate visit is the Colorado Ski Museum and Hall of Fame at 231 S. Frontage Road, 2 blocks east of I-70 Exit 176. In addition to explaining nearly everything there is to know about skiing and famous skiers, the museum covers the history of the area and the Tenth Mountain Division.

Getting There: Park close to the east end of the Vail Village parking structure. It has been free in past summers, but in the future there may be a small charge.

The Hike: Exit onto E. Meadow Drive and turn right (southeast) onto Vail Valley Drive. Cross it after 150 feet and take the asphalt path east along the north side of Gore Creek toward Ford Park. There is a bench at 0.06 mile. The path becomes dirt and gravel, and at 0.25 mile a sign points right to the Ford Amphitheater and the Alpine Gardens. At the Vail Recreation Program Office, turn left onto a path toward a children's playground. Continue on to the Betty Ford Alpine Gardens, reached at 0.39 mile. There are many benches here, and a series of rock steps leads to the top of the waterfalls. Pass through the Meditation Garden into the Mountain Perennial Garden, and at 0.60 mile exit the gardens and turn right (west). Note the Gore Creek Schoolhouse, built in 1922, at 0.62 mile. At 0.67 mile, pass a covered picnic area, and at 0.69 mile cross Gore Creek on a covered bridge.

At 0.80 mile, you can see the Golden Peak Ski Lift area to the left. Continue on Vail Valley Drive, which curves north, and at 0.98 mile turn left (west) onto Gore Creek Drive, which takes you past several condominiums and into a commercial district. At Bridge Street, turn left (south) and walk to the Vista Bahn ski area. Turn right at 1.21 miles onto Wall Street, descend some steps, and reach Gore Creek Drive again opposite the lovely Children's Fountain. Pass it on its west side and descend several steps to a path going west along the south side of Gore Creek.

At 1.37 miles, cross the creek on a bridge and reach Willow Bridge Road. Turn right and head to E. Meadow Drive, then turn left, again walking west. This puts you onto a mall where only buses are allowed. You will pass hotels and restaurants and, at 1.54 miles, the Vail Valley Tourist and Convention Bureau. Cross Vail Road at 1.56 miles onto W. Meadow Drive. Pass the fire department and

Betty Ford Alpine Gardens, Vail.

continue into a quiet area of homes and condominiums, reaching the Vail Valley Medical Center at 1.82 miles. At 1.83 miles, go left at a fork in the road onto a recreation path that parallels Gore Creek under a canopy of conifers. Cross a bridge over the creek, and just past a miniature golf course, come to the Born Free Express and Eagle Bahn Lionshead gondola at 1.92 miles.

Turn right at a bench and walk north to the Clock Tower Plaza. At the east side of the plaza, turn right again at 2.14 miles, pass several shops, and walk to the bus-stop area at E. Lionshead Circle. Continue heading east in front of the Lionshead parking structure and at 2.35 miles bear right, entering another road restricted to buses. At 2.39 miles, you will see the Dobson Ice Arena on the left and the Public Library on the right. Restrooms are located opposite the library entrance. Continue straight on W. Meadow Drive and then E. Meadow Drive to about the middle of the Vail Village parking structure. At 3.00 miles, turn right onto Bridge Street. Just before you reach the covered bridge, turn left onto the Gore Creek Stream Walk. This gravel path descends gently, passing a bench at 3.17 miles. The path ends at some steps up to Vail Valley Drive. Turn left and reenter the Vail Village parking garage at 3.18 miles.

49. Booth Falls

DEGREE OF DIFFICULTY: Hard
ROUND-TRIP DISTANCE: 4.08 miles
ROUND-TRIP TIME: 3 hours 5 minutes (1 hour 45 minutes up, 1 hour 20 minutes down)
STARTING ALTITUDE: 8,400 feet
ELEVATION GAIN: 1,400 feet
MAP: USGS Vail East

This hike's proximity to Vail, comparatively low altitude, and relatively short distance compared to other area hikes may fool people into expecting a leisurely expedition, a problem compounded by guidebooks that characterize the route as easy. We disagree. Even years ago, we struggled with its demands, which at times made us wonder whether we were close to exceeding our physical capacities. For seniors, this is likely to be a hard hike, particularly because of the very steep initial and final ascents, which also make for precipitous descents when one might well be fatigued. The views, however, do compensate to some extent for the effort expended.

Getting There: From the Vail entrance (Exit 176) onto I-70, drive east to Exit 180. At the stop sign at the bottom

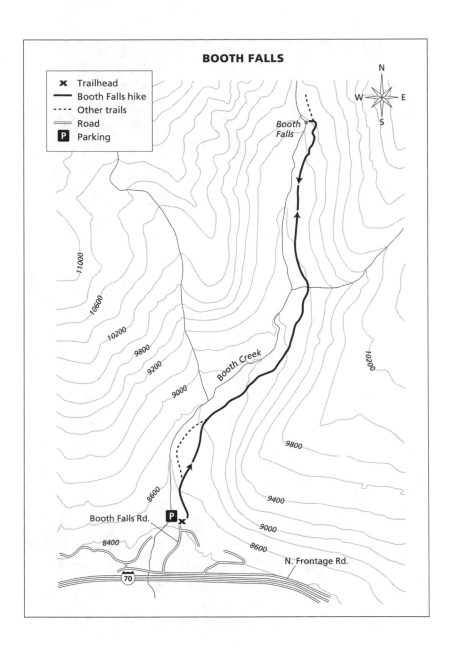

Lower portion of Booth Falls, Vail.

of the exit ramp, turn left and go west on N. Frontage Road for 1.0 mile. Turn right onto Booth Falls Road. Almost immediately, pass an overflow parking area on the right, adjacent to the Vail Mountain School. Continue up Booth Falls Road to a parking area for the trailhead at 0.21 mile. If this is full, which it often is, head back to the overflow parking area.

The Hike: Start at a gate at the north end of the parking lot and walk up a gravel road for a short distance to a signboard where there is a register. The dirt trail behind it ascends very steeply and at 0.06 mile switchbacks. As you ascend through aspen, look behind you for good views down the Vail Valley. Three more switchbacks lead to a sign at 0.26 mile indicating the Eagles Nest Wilderness Area/White River National Forest. The climb, now more gradual, cuts across a meadow. At 0.35 mile, enter an evergreen and aspen forest where the trail is wider but steeper. Reach some rocky steps at 0.43 mile. The trees are thin, allowing good views of the valley into which you are ascending. The Vail ski area is visible to the southwest.

In places, the trail is quite rocky. At 0.73 mile, enter an area of dense evergreens whose large roots cross the trail. Farther on, an aspen tree lies across the trail. At 0.89 mile, the valley opens up a bit, with Booth Creek on your left. Wildflowers, willows, and shrubs are located in an open meadow at 0.94 mile. Cross a creek at 1.04 miles and savor excellent views of the valley and the creek below. The trail gets steeper, dropping briefly to cross another small creek. At 1.37 miles, a short trail to the left affords a view into the gorge. Beyond this, the ascent gets even steeper, angling right at 1.78 miles. At times, you walk on loose rock.

The trail then alternates between steeper and flatter portions. Cross a small talus field at 1.96 miles.

At 1.99 miles, go left at a fork to a view point overlooking the bottom of the falls. Return to the main trail and continue your ascent. Turn left at 2.01 miles, passing through a stand of evergreens, and walk to the edge of the gorge. At 2.04 miles, there is a pleasant resting place under the trees, from which the upper portion of the falls is visible. Retrace your steps to the start, paying constant attention to the steep downhill grades.

50. Piney River Falls

DEGREE OF DIFFICULTY: Hard
ROUND-TRIP DISTANCE: 6.16 miles
ROUND-TRIP TIME: 3 hours 45 minutes (2 hours up, 1 hour 45 minutes down)
STARTING ALTITUDE: 9,360 feet
ELEVATION GAIN: 560 feet
MAPS: USGS Vail East, USGS Vail West

For more than 20 years, this was our favorite Vail-area hike. The views of the Gore Range are magnificent. The trail, which followed the Piney River up the middle of the valley, was easy to follow, and only in its final portion was the ascent very steep. In 2001, to our great surprise and dismay, the Forest Service rerouted most of the trail onto the valley's western slope to restore and protect the sensitive riparian area of the valley floor. The new hike avoids several of the lower marshy areas but is a bit longer and harder than the old one. Note that the April 1981 Forest Service description of Piney Lake gives its altitude as 9,360 feet, but their April 1993 description records it as 8,360 feet. Either the lake has sunk 1,000 feet or this is a misprint.

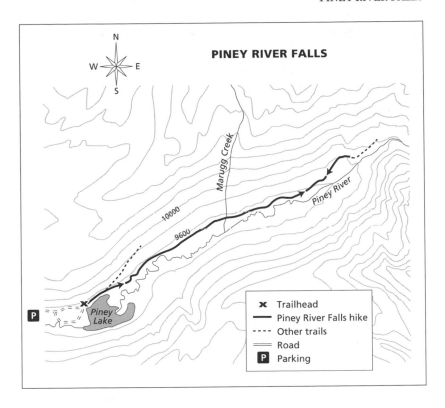

The 1970 USGS Vail West map records the lake altitude as 9,342 feet.

Getting There: From the traffic circle on N. Frontage Road off I-70 Exit 176, drive 1.0 mile west. At a sign indicating Piney Lake, turn right onto Red Sandstone Road. At 1.7 miles, go straight onto gravel County Road #700 at a sign for Piney River Ranch. At times, the road is a washboard, but cars can drive it without much difficulty. At 4.2 miles, Lost Lake Road goes off to the right. Continue straight, and at 8.2 miles pass a parking area for the Lost Lake Trail on your right. At 10.8 miles, cross a small bridge, and just beyond, turn right at a sign for Piney River Ranch. At 12.4 miles, reach a parking area just outside the ranch boundary. Signs warn that the ranch is private property. Public access paths begin just to the left of the gate and lead to the wilderness trail.

The Hike: Start at a brown Forest Service sign marking the trailhead and the public access path that heads northeast on a slope above the ranch. Piney Lake is visible at 0.21 mile. As you ascend gradually, Mt. Powell (13,534 feet) soon becomes visible at the upper end of the broad valley. Your route is joined by a lower trail coming in from the ranch at 0.41 mile. At 0.53 mile, reach a wilderness register and signboards for the Upper Piney River Trail. Pass through a horse gate and continue climbing gradually to the northeast. A sign at 0.60 mile announces the Eagles Nest Wilderness Area/White River National Forest.

Just beyond, another sign points to the new Upper Piney Trail #1885, which accesses Piney Falls and Upper Piney Lake. The old trail has been closed for revegetation. The trail ascends gradually, rising and dipping. At 0.75 mile, a sign points to the Marugg/Soda Lakes Trail #1889. Continue straight as the trail ascends and enter an aspen grove at 1.25 miles. You are now high above the valley. Cross a small creek at 1.43 miles, switchback to the southwest at 1.54 miles, and shortly switchback again to the northeast. At 1.64 miles, enter an evergreen area, in which you easily cross two creeks and a gully, making your way on logs with flattened surfaces. At 1.79 miles, the trail crosses a small meadow and soon re-enters an aspen grove. Switchback briefly to the southwest at 1.94 miles, then again to the northeast, and ascend more steeply. Six more short switchbacks

Piney River Valley, Vail.

Gore Range from Piney River Valley, Vail.

crossing several small creeks bring the trail into a clear area with a very steep dropoff to the right.

At 2.59 miles, the trail descends through four short switchbacks, crosses two small creeks, ascends again at 2.75 miles, traverses several more small wet and dry creeks, and descends again to wind under a large rock outcropping at 2.84 miles. Just beyond, a large boulder blocks the trail, forcing a steep descent and then a steep ascent back to the trail to get around it. Fortunately, in October 2001, a trail crew was preparing to blast a path through this rock, thus eliminating the difficult detour. The trail continues its ascent. At 2.92 miles, a small log (hopefully soon to be removed) lies across the trail. At 2.98 miles, the trail passes large rock outcroppings on the right and finally descends to the falls, reached at 3.08 miles. Although the falls at this point are not spectacular and the river is clogged with many dead tree branches, this is a pleasant spot in which to rest and enjoy a well-earned lunch.

Retrace your steps to the starting point. Be careful of your footing, since you may be more fatigued than you realize after this strenuous hike.

51. Shrine Ridge

DEGREE OF DIFFICULTY: Hard
ROUND-TRIP DISTANCE: 4.20 miles
ROUND-TRIP TIME: 3 hours 30 minutes (1 hour 50 minutes up, 1 hour 40 minutes down)
STARTING ALTITUDE: 11,089 feet
ELEVATION GAIN: 888 feet
MAPS: USGS Vail Pass, USGS Red Cliff

The views from the ridge top are some of the most spectacular we cover. This is also the highest hike in the book.

Shrine Ridge may have been named for a prominent 11,888-foot-high, eroded sandstone pillar just north of the ridge or for its excellent views of 14,005-foot-high Mount of the Holy Cross. The Ute knew of this area, for campsites and artifacts found during Vail Pass highway construction are said to date back 7,000 years. Shrine Pass Road, once a Native American trail, later carried traffic to Red Cliff at its southern end. Eventually, the Denver and Rio Grande Railroad came through here on its way to Glenwood Springs.

Getting There: From Vail Exit 176, drive 14.6 miles east on I-70 to Exit 190 at the Vail Pass Rest Area. Turn right onto the dirt Shrine Pass Road and continue 2.5 miles to a sign on the left for Shrine Ridge Trail parking. There are toilets across the road.

The Hike: From the parking lot, walk south on a wide dirt road to a gate at 0.06 mile where a sign announces that access is private. Another sign by the gate points left toward the Shrine Pass Trail. Still another sign on a pole marks the trail itself. Years ago, we used to go through the gate and up the road toward the Shrine Mountain Inn, accessing the trail nearby. That way is 0.20 mile longer round-trip and less scenic than the routing that follows.

Head down the Shrine Pass Trail. You will see a Shrine Pass sign on a pole at 0.10 mile. The trail, an old, rocky road, descends to cross a marshy meadow and a creek at 0.48 mile. At 0.51 mile, note the large pond created by a beaver dam. Cross a dry creek bed at 0.58 mile and begin a moderately steep ascent. A large cabin is visible off to the right at 0.71 mile. At 0.90 mile, a big log lies across the trail. At 0.93 mile, the trail that started near the inn comes in from the right, joining the one you are on.

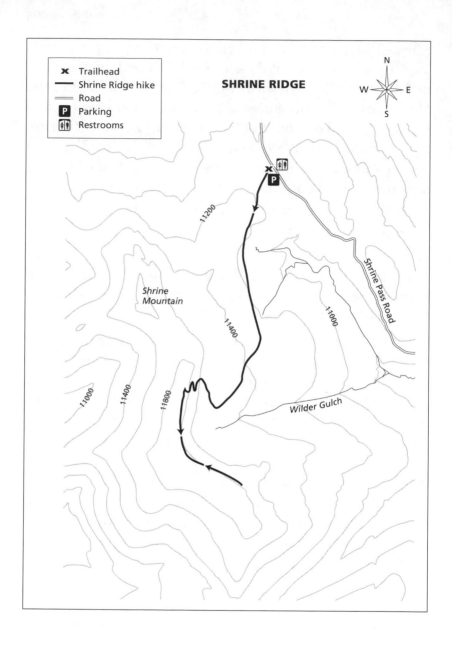

SHRINE RIDGE

Trailhead
Shrine Ridge hike
Road
P Parking
Restrooms

Shrine
Mountain

11200

11400

11000

11000

11400

11800

Wilder Gulch

Shrine Pass Road

Mount of the Holy Cross from Shrine Ridge, Vail.

The trail now curves southwest and at 1.05 miles passes through an area of tree stumps created by logging operations and wildfire. The views to the north and east are impressive. Circle around a large log at 1.20 miles and enter a conifer forest shortly thereafter. Many roots cross the trail here. Exit the woods at 1.39 miles. Shrine Ridge rises in front of you. The trail parallels it going west, and for a time the ascent is less steep. This changes at 1.50 miles, where the path becomes quite rocky. The trail passes to the left of a ridge pole with a cairn at 1.67 miles. Pass another cairn with a blue ridge marker at 1.74 miles. At this point, it is likely to be quite windy since you are now on the exposed ridge.

At 1.75 miles, the trail splits. Both forks go to the ridge top, but we usually take the right one. They come together shortly before the saddle (1.85 miles), which offers incredible views to the north, east, and west. Two cairns are located here. Continue to ascend past stunted and twisted evergreens at 1.88 miles. The view of the Mount of the Holy Cross to the southwest is terrific. At 1.96 miles, go right at a fork and ascend steeply. Shrine Pass Road is now visible to the northeast. Turn left at a fork at 1.98 miles and immediately left again. Just beyond is the best view of the Mount of the Holy Cross.

Retrace your steps to the fork and turn left to ascend the steep trail to the ridge top at 2.10 miles. From here, you can see Shrine Mountain to the north-northeast, Uneva Peak (12,522 feet) to the east-northeast, the Sawatch Range to the southwest, and Mt. Massive (14,421 feet) to the south. Descend the way you came.

Boulder

Created in 1975, Boulder County Parks and Open Space now manages approximately 50,000 acres of land. Hiking trails exist in 14 of the 17 named Open Space areas. We have hiked many trails in the foothills area between 5,500 and 8,500 feet and have been impressed with the steep ascents that characterize some of them. For this book, we have chosen a representative group that are appropriate for seniors and can serve as an introduction to this region for those who wish to attempt additional hikes. Many of the trails are extremely hot in summer; spring and fall are usually the best times to go. Unlike the Jefferson County Open Space system, toilet facilities in the Boulder County system are few and far between. Mileage to trailheads is measured from the intersection of Broadway and Baseline Road in Boulder.

52. Sanitas Valley and Dakota Ridge Trails

DEGREE OF DIFFICULTY: Sanitas Valley Trail—Easy;
  Dakota Ridge Trail—Moderate
ROUND-TRIP DISTANCE: 2.18 miles
ROUND-TRIP TIME: 1 hour 30 minutes
STARTING ALTITUDE: 5,520 feet
ELEVATION GAIN: 440 feet
Maps: Boulder Mountain Park Trail Map, Mt. Sanitas
  brochure

In 1895, Seventh-Day Adventists established a sanitarium for general medical and tuberculosis care near what is now the Mt. Sanitas Trailhead. The name "Mt. Sanitas" (from the Latin word for health) pays tribute to this medical facility. Though a hike to the summit (6,863 feet) is quite steep, and for older hikers very strenuous, the valley hike is much easier. The Valley Trail (accessible by wheelchair) runs up a gravel road that in the past served as a wagon access to quarries on Mt. Sanitas and, later, as a fire road. Returning down the narrower, rocky Dakota Ridge Trail through ponderosa pines provides more of a mountain hiking experience.

One writer has called the Sanitas Valley "canine heaven," and you are indeed likely to encounter a large number of dogs and runners on the Valley Trail. Fortunately, it is wide enough to accommodate all comers without seeming crowded. Years ago, this area served as rangeland for cattle.

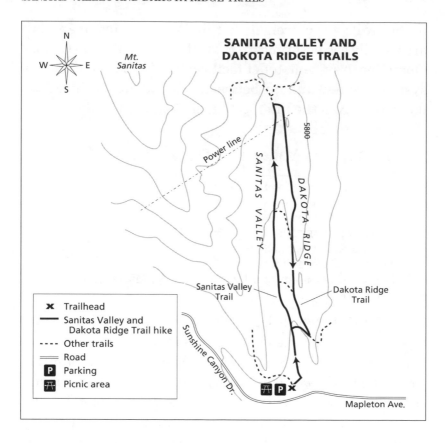

Quarries on Mt. Sanitas owned and operated by the University of Colorado in the 1920s provided the Lyons sandstone from which several university buildings were constructed. When the quarries later became unprofitable, they were purchased by the City of Boulder as part of its Open Space system.

Mt. Sanitas and Dakota Ridge consist of narrow, parallel ridges (hogbacks) of sedimentary rock elevated and

View of Sanitas Valley from Dakota Ridge Trail, Boulder.

tilted during uplifts millions of years ago. The valley between them resulted from erosion of the softer rock and soil material.

This area reflects the junction of the Great Plains grasslands and the shrubs and forests of the Rocky Mountain foothills. On a recent early May hike, we identified a variety of prairie grasses, prickly pear cactus (women should take care when making a pit stop [no toilets are available]), yucca, sand lilies, mouse-ear chickweed, larkspur, mountain yarrow, chiming bells, buttercups, and blue flax.

Getting There: From the intersection of Broadway and Baseline Road, go north on Broadway for 1.8 miles to Mapleton Avenue. Turn left (west), pass the Boulder Community Hospital Mapleton Center on the right, and at 2.7

miles (the mouth of Sunshine Canyon) park in one of two small parking areas on the right identified by a Mt. Sanitas Trailhead parking sign. A larger parking area is 0.1 mile farther on the left.

The Hike: From the parking area, head north down five steps to a covered picnic area. A signboard with a map and brochures is located here. Cross a bridge over a stream. At approximately 100 feet, a signpost indicates the Mt. Sanitas Trail up and to the left and the Sanitas Valley Trail—the one you want—up and to the right. Ascend a series of steps to join a wide dirt trail. At 0.06 mile, go left, ignoring a trail to the right. At 0.08 mile, a signpost points to the wide, gravel Sanitas Valley Trail. Just beyond is an information signboard.

Gradually ascend north up the valley, with Mt. Sanitas to the left and Dakota Ridge to the right. At 0.22 mile, a signpost indicates the Dakota Ridge Trail to the right. Ignore this and continue up the road, from which you can see mine openings and tailings on Mt. Sanitas. At 0.60 mile, another signpost indicates access to the Dakota Ridge Trail on the right. Again, continue up the valley. Houses are visible on the left at the head of the valley.

At 0.99 mile, a trail to the right leads to another signpost identifying the Dakota Ridge Trail, which you will take. Just beyond, at 1.00 mile, there is an observation point with an excellent view of Boulder. The Hawthorne Trail heads down into the gully ahead of you, and the East Ridge Trail runs off to the left to join the Mt. Sanitas Trail. This is a good place for a picnic.

Descend on the trail along the west side of Dakota Ridge. The route provides excellent views of Mt. Sanitas and the valley. At 1.04 miles, there is a short stretch of fence on your left. The descent varies between gradual and steep and passes under a power line at 1.08 miles. An evergreen forest shades this area. At times, the trail is rocky and care is required. You are high over the Sanitas Valley, with a good view of the foothills. A great many birds sing here. At 1.51 miles, there is a lot of loose rock underfoot; a sign at this point denotes the Dakota Ridge Trail. Another signpost at 1.56 miles indicates access to the Sanitas Valley Trail on the right. Continue straight down the Dakota Ridge Trail, pass another Dakota Ridge Trail signpost at 1.58 miles, and at 1.71 miles go down a steep set of steps. Turn left at a signpost at the bottom. At 1.85 miles, the right side of the trail is fenced. At 1.89 miles, turn right and descend to the Sanitas Valley Trail, which you will reach at 1.96 miles. Turn left and at 2.10 miles turn right at a sign indicating the Mt. Sanitas Trail. End at the parking lot at 2.18 miles.

53. Enchanted Mesa/McClintock Nature Trails

DEGREE OF DIFFICULTY: Easy
ROUND-TRIP DISTANCE: 1.79 miles
ROUND-TRIP TIME: 1 hour 15 minutes
STARTING ALTITUDE: 5,730 feet
ELEVATION GAIN: 430 feet
MAP: Boulder Mountain Parks brochure

This loop is only one of many labyrinthine trails in the Chautauqua Park/Boulder Mountain Park area. Chautauqua Park and its auditorium were established in 1898 on an 80-acre site on the east slope of Flagstaff Mountain. The park sits at the northern end of the Mesa Trail, which wanders more than 6 miles one way to its southern trailhead

near Eldorado Springs. The short loop that we describe offers good views of the plains and the Flatirons. The latter, part of the Fountain Formation, are similar to slabs found in Red Rocks Park near Denver and the Garden of the Gods near Colorado Springs. The Flatirons tilted into their present position during uplifts approximately 135 and 63 million years ago. Erosion over time has exposed them to view.

Getting There: From the intersection of Broadway and Baseline Road, go west on Baseline 0.8 mile to 12th Street. Turn left, go 0.1 mile to Columbine Street, then turn right and go past Chautauqua Auditorium 0.2 mile to a parking lot. Several benches and picnic tables are adjacent. If this lot is full, there is another parking lot just before the auditorium, and an overflow lot just before that.

The Hike: At the southeast corner of the first parking lot, there is a signboard with a Boulder Mountain Parks map. At the gate beyond it, begin hiking up a wide, dirt fire road with the Flatirons ahead to the south. The ascent is gentle, with Bluebell Creek on the left. At 0.14 mile, cross a stone bridge over the stream to a sign indicating the Enchanted Mesa Trail to the left and the McClintock Trail to the right. Go left and ignore another sign noting the McClintock Trail to the left at 0.16 mile.

The trail ascends gently to the east, offering views of the plains and mountains, as well as Chautauqua Auditorium. At 0.33 mile, ignore a short access road to the right, which goes to the base of the covered city reservoir. Enjoy a lovely view of Boulder, the University of Colorado, and the plains to the east (left). The trail now curves to the right past views of several spectacular homes. The Flatirons and the reservoir are visible as well. Ignore another access road to the right. At 0.47 mile, arrive at another signboard with a map, and if you look back, the entire roof of the reservoir is visible. Just behind the signboard, a short trail to the left leads to another overlook.

Continue ascending toward the Flatirons through an area of widely spaced evergreens, passing a trail to the right at 0.60 mile. At 0.92 mile, a signpost indicates the

Flatirons from Enchanted Mesa Trail, Boulder.

Kohler Mesa North Trail to the left. Just opposite is an unmarked trail heading right. Leave the Enchanted Mesa Trail for this narrow, unmarked one, which ascends to the north. Cross a log at 0.96 mile, ignore trails to the right and left at 1.05 miles, and at 1.10 miles intersect the wide Mesa Trail (different from the Enchanted Mesa Trail), also unmarked at this point. Go right, and descend to a sign at 1.17 miles telling you that you have been on the Mesa Trail. The sign also identifies the McClintock Trail; turn right and descend on this. Many signs along the way describe the area's flora and fauna, as well as the city and climate. Descend a flight of steps at 1.19 miles and walk alongside a gully on your left. This path is steep and deserves care, particularly if it is wet. The auditorium is visible at 1.43

miles. Shortly thereafter, the trail forks. Bear left. At 1.63 miles, regain the Enchanted Mesa Trail at the stone bridge, go left on the fire road, and reach the starting point at 1.79 miles.

54. Bald Mountain Loop

> DEGREE OF DIFFICULTY: Easy
> ROUND-TRIP DISTANCE: 1.10 miles
> ROUND-TRIP TIME: 40 minutes
> STARTING ALTITUDE: 6,920 feet
> ELEVATION GAIN: 240 feet
> MAPS: Bald Mountain Scenic Area brochure, USGS Gold Hill

We include this short, easy, and very pleasant hike in the 108-acre Bald Mountain Scenic Area, opened in 1973, for its spectacular view of the Indian Peaks and Continental Divide to the west. The mountain earned its name because the coarse, shallow soils on its summit do not retain moisture well. This, in addition to high, evaporative winds and dry summer heat, leads to restricted tree growth, giving the mountain its "bald" appearance. Granodiorite, an igneous rock formed from molten material 1.7 billion years ago, provides a solid core for Bald Mountain. Cattle grazing began here in 1886; 10 years later a fruitless search for valuable minerals started.

Getting There: From the intersection of Broadway and Baseline Road, go north on Broadway for 1.8 miles to Mapleton Avenue. Turn left (west) on Mapleton, pass Boulder Community Hospital Mapleton Center on the right, and enter Sunshine Canyon. The road is steep and winding. At 5.1 miles from the turn onto Mapleton, enter the large Bald Mountain Scenic Area parking lot on the left. A portable toilet is located here.

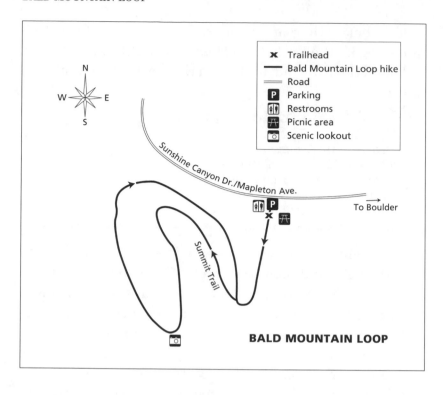

N
W · E
S

✖	Trailhead
▬	Bald Mountain Loop hike
═	Road
🅿	Parking
🚻	Restrooms
⛏	Picnic area
📷	Scenic lookout

Sunshine Canyon Dr./Mapleton Ave.

To Boulder

Summit Trail

BALD MOUNTAIN LOOP

The Hike: From the west side of the parking lot, five steps lead up to the trail, where there is a signboard and brochures. Proceed south on a wide, dirt path through a picnic area with tables and grills. Ignore a trail coming in from the left at 0.06 mile. A sign here reminds you that this is mountain lion habitat and suggests how to handle an encounter. There is a good view of the foothills to the east.

The trail continues through widely spaced ponderosa pines, becoming steeper. Note the private property sign on the left at 0.13 mile, just before a switchback to the northwest. A sign at 0.14 mile indicates the Summit Trail to the left and the Pines to Peaks Trail to the right. Turn left onto the Summit Trail. At 0.21 mile, the wide trail is steep and rocky. The peaks of the Continental Divide are clearly visible at 0.28 mile. Continue toward a bench on the summit at 0.36 mile. There is a 360-degree view of the Continental Divide to the west, the plains to the east, and the foothills all around.

Continue southeast, descending on a wider, smoother path that becomes steeper at 0.41 mile. Ignore a path to the left that leads to a private property sign and gate. The path curves west and again offers a wonderful view of the peaks on the Divide. A bench is located at 0.55 mile. At 0.62 mile, a 60-foot path leads to a rocky outcrop with a view into a canyon. Continue west on the main path, which descends gradually. At 0.72 mile, the wide trail parallels the highway for a bit and re-enters the trees at 0.78 mile. At 0.96 mile, the sign you encountered previously alerts you to the fact that you have been descending on the Pines to Peaks Trail. The trail heads down and to the left at 0.97 mile. At 1.04 miles, go right through the picnic ground to the parking area.

55. Green Mountain West Ridge Trail

DEGREE OF DIFFICULTY: Hard
ROUND-TRIP DISTANCE: 2.80 miles
ROUND-TRIP TIME: 2 hours 40 minutes (1 hour 40 minutes up, 1 hour down)
STARTING ALTITUDE: 7,544 feet
ELEVATION GAIN: 600 feet
MAPS: Boulder Mountain Parks and Nearby Open Space Trail Map, City of Boulder Open Space and Mountain Parks Lands Trails Map

Green Mountain (8,144 feet) is known as a "must" hike in the Boulder area because of the fine view it affords of

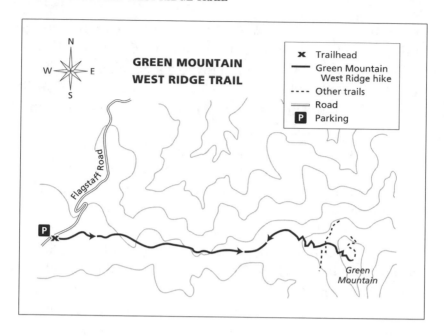

the Front Range. Several routes lead to the summit, but most are long and gain 1,350–2,850 feet in elevation. The West Ridge Trail is the shortest and easiest (relatively) of these paths. Though this may not be a difficult hike for young people (we met one woman on the trail who did it daily), it is a hard but worthwhile hike for seniors. The trailhead is difficult to find, indicating that this route may not be as popular as other routes that approach the mountain from the north.

Only roadside parking is available near the trailhead. Most cars park just beyond the Boulder Mountain Parks boundary; this way, they do not need a parks permit. However, we suspect that it would be safer to buy a vehicle permit ($3 daily, $15 annually) rather than risk a $25 fine for vehicles not registered in Boulder County. In addition, these permits allow parking at many other interesting locations on Flagstaff Road, where they may be purchased.

Getting There: At the intersection of Baseline Road and Broadway, go west up Baseline for 1.2 miles to 6th Street and Baseline Road, beyond which Baseline becomes Flagstaff Road. From 6th and Baseline, drive 5.0 more miles up Flagstaff Mountain on steep and winding Flagstaff Road. The trailhead, on the left, is set back from the road and easy to miss. If you reach Kossler Lake, you have gone too far. The landmark to watch for at 5.0 miles is a sign on the left that says "Leaving City of Boulder Mountain Parks" on its north side. Park off the road just opposite or near this sign without obstructing several private drives nearby.

The trailhead sign is 45 feet east of the highway. Just beyond it is a signboard with a parks map. Driving up, the only toilet we found was on the right just beyond the Lost Gulch Overlook and just before the Cathedral Park Picnic Area about 0.5 mile before the trailhead.

The Hike: The trail heads east, with minor deviations north and south. At first, it dips and rises while passing through a parklike area of widely spaced evergreens. At 0.18 mile, the trail gets rockier. A signpost at 0.20 mile identifies the Green Mountain West Ridge Trail. It descends a bit as it crosses a slope at 0.26 mile. You are now shaded by denser evergreens. At 0.31 mile, ascend again on a narrow and moderately steep path. At 0.37 mile, reach a multistrand wire boundary fence on the right, paralleling a dirt road. The trail goes up and down, sometimes in the open, sometimes in a dense forest.

Cairn on top of Green Mountain, Boulder.

The descent is steeper at 0.53 mile, with a good view of the plains to the left. At the bottom, you will find wooden posts connected by fence wire. Ascend again, noting the three-tiered house ahead to the right. Green Mountain is in front of you; to the west are the peaks of the Continental Divide, from Longs Peak south to James Peak. The trail is rockier at 0.70 mile, then descends gently to a meadow. Reach a signpost marking the trail at 0.76 mile, after which the route follows an old road. The meadows are full of wildflowers and songbirds. As you ascend, the trail becomes steeper and rockier. Go up some steps at 1.10 miles. Just beyond, the trail switchbacks toward the east.

At 1.20 miles, there is a signpost on each side of the trail. The Ranger Trail goes to the left, the Green Bear

Trail to the right. Continue straight on the Green Mountain West Ridge Trail. The ascent is now much steeper. At 1.28 miles, climb a flight of steps, enjoying views of James Peak and the Eldora ski area. The trail is even rockier now, but white blazes on trees keep you oriented. At 1.34 miles, note the Green Mountain West Ridge Trail marker on a tree to the left. The trail curves a bit back and forth but heads predominantly east. Switchback at 1.35 miles, where you will see another trail marker on a tree.

Ascend another steep, rocky set of steps. At 1.39 miles, pause under a huge boulder with a cairn on it marking the summit. You can go straight up the slope to the right or bear left around the boulder to reach a flat area at 1.40 miles, just below the cairn. The marker on top of the cairn identifies some of the Continental Divide peaks. At the north end of the flat area is a Greenman Trail signpost. The view of Boulder to the east is impressive.

Return the way you came. Exercise extreme care going down the rocky stretches and use the white blazes on the trees to keep yourself oriented to the trail. Recognize that when you are fatigued, you tend not to lift your feet as high when walking, increasing your likelihood of tripping.

56. Sugarloaf Mountain

DEGREE OF DIFFICULTY: Moderate
ROUND-TRIP DISTANCE: 1.34 miles
ROUND-TRIP TIME: 1 hour (35 minutes up, 25 minutes down)
STARTING ALTITUDE: 8,441 feet
ELEVATION GAIN: 476 feet
MAP: USGS Gold Hill

There is an impressive 360-degree view from the top of this nearly denuded 8,917-foot peak in the Roosevelt Na-

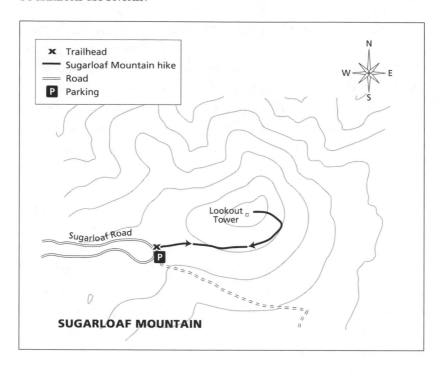

tional Forest. Looking northwest and moving south along the Continental Divide, you can easily identify Longs Peak, Mt. Audubon, Arapaho Peak and its glacier, the Eldora ski area, and James Peak. They were beautifully snowcapped in May 2001. The Great Plains stretch to the east, the foothills and Front Range to the south. For this hike, park along the old Switzerland Trail on what was once the track bed of the Greeley, Salt Lake and Pacific Narrow Gauge Railroad (1883) and later the Colorado and Northwestern Railroad (1898). From Boulder, the tracks ran west and then northwest to many of the area's gold-mining towns, among them Crisman, Ward, and Sunset. Floods eventually wiped

Sugarloaf Mountain, Boulder.

out both railroads. The Sugarloaf community was established even earlier, in 1860.

In 1988, lightning started a fire that burned much of the evergreen forest covering Sugarloaf Mountain. The top of the trail runs through this area, which is recovering slowly. Few people take this hike up a scree-covered old mining road, although young people in four-wheel-drive vehicles sometimes party so loudly that the Sheriff's Department is called out. We consider this short but steep hike highly worthwhile, but it does require caution and careful footing on the loose rock, especially on the descent.

Getting There: From the intersection of Broadway and Baseline Road, go north on Broadway 1.5 miles to Canyon Boulevard (Colorado Highway 119). Turn left and go west on Highway 119 for 5.4 miles, just past a sign for Sugarloaf Road. Make a sharp right turn and ascend steep, paved Sugarloaf Road, which soon enters the Roosevelt National Forest. After an additional 4.9 miles, turn right onto the unpaved Sugarloaf Mountain Road, where a sign indicates the Switzerland Trail 1.0 mile ahead and Sunset Townsite 5.0 miles ahead. The road is bumpy but otherwise good. Reach a large unpaved parking area 0.8 mile down this road, where there is a sign indicating the Switzerland Trail, Sunset Townsite 5.0 miles to the right, and Glacier Lake 6.0 miles to the left.

The Hike: Walk to the north end of the parking area, where there is a superb view of Longs Peak straight ahead. Just to the right is an unmarked dirt road that ascends to the east. This is the route you will take. Not far down the road is a wire barrier; the hike is measured from this point. (We have also started the hike at the southeast corner of the parking lot on another access road, which is blocked by a gate with a "No Parking, Emergency Access Only" sign, but we do not recommend it, as the ascent is much steeper.)

The trail is very rocky and steep. When possible, walk on the edge, where there is less loose rock. At 0.03 mile, ignore a fork to the right, which will rejoin the main trail higher up. Pass through the residual evergreen forest. At 0.26 mile, switchback to the north. The burned-out area now becomes more visible, as do the peaks of the Continental Divide to the west. Switchback again to the east at 0.33 mile, where the views west become even more spectacular. Reach a Sugarloaf Mountain regulations sign at 0.40 mile.

The ascent gets steeper. The view down into the valley, crisscrossed by roads and dotted with houses, is worth a pause. At 0.51 mile, there is a large charred tree trunk still standing on the left side of the road. The trail is now rockier as it ascends through the burned-out area, crossing the face of the mountain. If there is no wind, this stretch of trail can be quite hot. Arrive at the windswept, relatively flat summit at 0.67 mile. It makes an excellent picnic spot to enjoy the surrounding panorama. Retrace your steps with care to the parking area.

Index

Page numbers in italics indicate illustrations.
Page numbers in bold indicate hike listings.